Praise for *Pulling Harvey Out of Her Hat*

"A very enjoyable and interesting story that needs to be told."—**David Forsyth**, Clear Creek County historian

"A well-researched and detailed biography of Pulitzer Prize–winner Mary Chase. Her beloved play, *Harvey*, written in 1944, is still being produced today in theatres around the world."—**Joanna H. Kraus**, playwright, professor emerita, State University of New York

"The shallow thought Mary Chase just sought to entertain with *Harvey* as an escapist fantasy. Hidden behind the surface was an acute critic with a larger vision and message. Mimi Pockross begins to peak behind the scenes in this much needed book."—**Phil Goodstein**, historian to the author of *Modern East Denver*

"*Pulling Harvey Out of Her Hat* is a warm and informative story of Denverite Mary Coyle Chase who wrote the endearing and inspirational play *Harvey* that is known and loved by generations of American theater and movie lovers." —**Georgianna Contiguglia**, past president and CEO of History Colorado

"Mimi Pockross has created a warm and human profile of playwright Mary Coyle Chase, author of the stage and screen comedy classic *Harvey*. Pockross's biography provides a lovingly detailed vision of how Chase tenaciously persevered at her craft and eventually succeeded writ large, adding to the American comedic canon at a time when few women were able or permitted to do so." —**Andrew Erdman**, author of *Queen of Vaudeville: The Story of Eva Tanguay*

"A charming, intimate portrait of Denver playwright Mary Coyle Chase . . . weaves history into the narrative to give the necessary perspective on the era in which Chase's blockbuster *Harvey* was written and further explores far beyond the *Harvey* narrative in detailed explanation of the totality of Chase's work including her extensive efforts with children's plays."—**Cle Cervi Symons**, publisher of the *Cervi Journal*

PULLING
HARVEY
OUT OF
HER HAT

PULLING
HARVEY
OUT OF
HER HAT

THE AMAZING STORY OF
Mary Coyle Chase

MIMI POCKROSS

ROWMAN & LITTLEFIELD
Lanham • Boulder • New York • London

Published by Rowman & Littlefield
An imprint of The Rowman & Littlefield Publishing Group, Inc.
4501 Forbes Boulevard, Suite 200, Lanham, Maryland 20706
www.rowman.com

6 Tinworth Street, London SE11 5AL, United Kingdom

British Library Cataloguing in Publication Information Available

Library of Congress Cataloging-in-Publication Data
Names: Pockross, Mimi, author.
Title: Pulling Harvey out of her hat : the amazing story of Mary Coyle Chase /
   Mimi Pockross.
Description: Lanham : A Limelight Edition/Rowman & Littlefield, [2020] |
   Includes bibliographical references and index. | Summary: "The true story of how
   playwright Mary Chase hopped to fame, fortune, and a Pulitzer Prize—all while
   raising her family and working as a reporter in Denver, Colorado"—Provided
   by publisher.
Identifiers: LCCN 2020028036 (print) | LCCN 2020028037 (ebook) |
   ISBN 9781538131688 (cloth) | ISBN 9781538131695 (epub)
Subjects: LCSH: Chase, Mary, 1907–1981. | Dramatists, American—20th century—
   Biography.
Classification: LCC PS3505.H478 Z83 2020 (print) | LCC PS3505.H478 (ebook) |
   DDC 812/.52 [B]—dc23
LC record available at https://lccn.loc.gov/2020028036
LC ebook record available at https://lccn.loc.gov/2020028037

To Harvey and to my friend Clara

How you climb a mountain is more important than reaching the top.

—YVON CHOUINARD

CONTENTS

Act III. After *Harvey*

PREFACE

My love of theater began when I was nine and my mother signed up my brother and me to take drama lessons with a woman named Irene Kramsky. One of my earliest memories is the introduction she gave us to radio drama. We learned how to make all the kinds of sound effects that Garrison Keillor later created on his program *A Prairie Home Companion*. This was just the beginning of a love affair with the theater that ultimately led me to be interested in writing a book about Mary Chase.

There are so many people to thank for bringing this book to life.

First and foremost I would like to thank Carol Flannery, my acquisitions editor at Rowman & Littlefield, for reaching out to me, for recognizing Mary Chase's importance, and for guiding me along in telling this story; and to Mary Anne Maier who helped me with my original proposal.

Perhaps the highlight for me was my conversation with Jerry Chase and his wife, Mary. It was a thrill to speak to them.

I would never have been able to be as accurate or thought-provoking without the assistance of Phil Goodstein, "Mister Denver," the author of more than twenty books.

I am especially grateful to Michael Ditchfield, who introduced me to Georgia Garnsey who introduced me to Clé Cervi Symons, and to my cousin Barbara Goldburg who introduced me to Susan and the late Tom Hilb. Interviews with Symons and the Hilbs were both revealing and totally enjoyable. Thanks also to my cousins Mimi Rotter and Nancy Simon for their input.

I was lucky to be able to communicate with many other Mary Chase fans along the way: Colorado historians Dave Forsyth, Tom Noel, and Stephen Leonard; the employees of Central City Opera Association and especially the administrator, Wanda Larson; New York University emeritus professor Joanna Kraus; and authors Andrew Erdman and Laura Shamas.

Thanks to everyone at the Denver Public Library, especially Abby Hoverstock and Coi Drummond-Gehrig; to the University of Denver Special Collections librarian Katherine Crowe; to Robert Freedman for his wonderful conversations; to Patrick Hederman, Jed Feffer, and Marianne Merola; to Ben Harry; to the Houghton Library at Harvard University; and to the Billy Rose Theatre Division of the New York Library for the Performing Arts.

And lastly but most importantly, to my wonderful family who always support and inspire me: to my sons and their wives, my delightful grandchildren, and especially to my husband, Keith, for his insight, his humor, and his patience.

To learn about this gifted playwright has been a special treat and privilege. I hope that her story will enrich every theater lover and will bring new followers to the fore.

INTRODUCTION

Her Life Changed Forever

On the evening of November 1, 1944, Bob and Mary Chase from Denver, Colorado, took their seats in the front row of the 48th Street Theater in New York City to watch the debut of *Harvey*, a tale about the friendship of an aging alcoholic by the name of Elwood P. Dowd and his imaginary friend, a six-foot, one-and-a-half-inch rabbit named Harvey.

The playwright of this debut was a stylishly attired woman dressed in a fashionable black silk dress: Mary Coyle Chase, aged thirty-seven. Her handsome companion was her husband, Bob, a hard-driving news editor at the *Rocky Mountain News* and the father of their three young sons whom they had left at home under the care of the couple's friends and family.

Chase tried not to think about a similar scenario that she had experienced seven years before. Why she had decided to put herself through this effort once more did not seem clear to her as she sat and watched the house fill up with theatergoers.

On her mind as well were her worries about her husband's and her finances. Providing for three young children and keeping herself in style on the salary of a young journalist had its difficulties. In fact, she and her husband had had to borrow three hundred dollars just to get to New York to attend the opening.

Chase convinced herself that after tonight her dream to dwell in a mansion such as those that were occupied by her millionaire neighbors would no longer be her goal in life. She was going to put her aspirations on hold and go back to raising her children and writing newsletters.

The audience quieted down and the curtain rose on a comfortable living room furnished with dulling chandeliers and aging paneled woodwork where the two ladies of the house, Veta Louise Simmons and her spinster daughter, Myrtle Mae, huddled together and discussed their worries about the possibility of Veta's eccentric brother making an appearance at the tea for the society ladies they were currently hosting in the parlor directly offstage.

From the moment when the curtain rose on *Harvey*, Chase's life would change forever.

ACT I

Harvey Begins

In her lifetime, Mary Chase authored fourteen published plays, three screenplays, and two award-winning children's books. Chase's play *Harvey* received the Pulitzer Prize for Drama in 1945.

Born of humble roots to immigrant Irish parents, Chase from the onset had a burning desire to stand out in the crowd. She was bright, beautiful, rebellious, passionate, and determined to get what she wanted.

Chase possessed a lively imagination and an unlimited curiosity to learn about others, and her early life experiences laid the groundwork for the enduring stories she would later tell.

I

THE COYLES AND
THE McDONOUGHS

MEET THE PARENTS

Mary Coyle arrived in the world on February 25, 1907.* She was the fourth and last child born to Frank and Mary McDonough Coyle.

Frank's parents were Irish immigrants who came to America to escape the potato famines that had begun in 1845 and had continually persisted. The Coyles settled in Illinois, but Frank moved to Oklahoma after word spread in the late 1800s that gold deposits had been discovered there. When that rumor proved not to be true, Frank again moved on, this time to Denver where he settled in the Irish neighborhood of West Denver.[1]

Chase's mother arrived in Denver around the same time as her future husband. Her four brothers had left County Tyrone in northern Ireland in the late 1800s and had first headed to Cripple Creek, Colorado, to look for that elusive gold. After their quest was also unsuccessful, they too moved on to Denver where work was more available for laborers. The uncles then asked their sister to come across the seas to take care of them. She arrived at the age of sixteen and she too settled in West Denver.[2]

Both parents joined the wave of Irish immigrants who continued to arrive well into the late nineteenth century and to answer the growing need for laborers.[3]

Chase's parents first met at the Catholic convent where her mother attended school and her father delivered groceries. They married in 1898 and settled down to raise a family in the same area where they had met.

---

*A dispute exists as to whether Chase was born in 1906 or 1907 that goes back to the date she listed when applying for her marriage license. The date listed on her tombstone is February 25, 1906.

Frank found employment as a salesman for the Hungarian Flour Milling and Elevator Company, a job he held for the duration of his working life. John Mullen, another Irish immigrant, owned the company. Mullen had brought the Hungarian process of milling to Denver and was an important political figure in the city.

In quick succession, a daughter, Katherine, was born, followed by two boys, Frank and Charlie. Nine years later in 1907 another daughter, Mary Agnes McDonough Coyle, was born. From the beginning she was feisty, brash, and contrary.

The Coyles lived in one of the modest buildings of West Denver, a crowded area of apartments and small houses. Frank Coyle wanted to protect his growing family and find a quieter and more refined neighborhood where they could live. He managed to save fifty dollars for a down payment on a twenty-five hundred dollar home in an area of town that later became known as the Baker neighborhood.[4] In 1907 the family moved to 532 West Fourth Avenue where Mary Chase lived until after she married and gave birth to her second child.

Chase's neighborhood was considered middle class and edged up to the more upscale Capitol Hill area where Mrs. Crawford Hill, a leading member of the community and a member of the prestigious Sacred Thirty-Six Society, resided. Chase's house was in the middle of the block among the smaller houses. It was a two-story house with seven rooms. The corner houses on the street were larger and more desirable.

Despite the fact that most of the houses were modest, each was unique and individual. The homes in the neighborhood were primarily built in the Queen Anne style that was popular at the time. They possessed gabled roofs and wide front porches, and they were decorated with gingerbread ornamentation on their facades. In 1985 the Baker district was listed on the National Register of Historic Homes for its preservation of the largest number of Queen Anne style homes. The Coyle home became a designated Denver landmark in 1975.

The neighborhood was characterized as having a vertical population whose occupants held a variety of vocations and income levels. Among the residents who lived near the Coyles were a surgeon, a physician, Denver's first police matron, Colorado's first poet laureate, and musicians Wilberforce Whiteman and his wife, Elfrida. The Whitemans' son Paul became a nationally known bandleader.[5]

There were ten residents in the Coyle home: Chase's mother; her father; her two brothers; her sister; her four uncles, Timothy, James, Peter, and John; and Chase. A small shed in the back housed the horse and buggy that Frank hooked up each day when he made the rounds to see his flour mill accounts.

THE HOMETOWN

By the time Mary Chase was born in 1907, Denver, Colorado, had become a vibrant and increasingly diverse city with a population of two hundred thousand. The Denver of Chase's time served as a background for many of her plays.

In *Harvey*, the Pulitzer Prize play that she wrote in 1944, Elwood P. Dowd lives in a town resembling Denver. His house looks like a mansion in Capitol Hill where many of Denver's wealthiest families dwelt. Elwood and Harvey meet by a lamppost in a middle-class neighborhood similar to one where the Chase family lived when Chase married, and Harvey and Elwood stop for a drink at a bar similar to the one that her uncles often patronized near her childhood home. In *Me Third*, Chase's first entry onto the Broadway scene, her play chronicles political corruption in a mid-sized city patterned after events she had observed as a newspaper reporter in Denver. And in *Mrs. McThing*, Chase highlights the division between those who live in an upper-class neighborhood like Denver's Capitol Hill and those who reside in crime-ridden Shantyland, a part of town similar to some of the poorer areas Chase covered when she was a news reporter.

Most people call Denver a cosmopolitan city, but many still concede that the label of "cow town" was attached for good reason. After all, this was a town that grew up during the waning days of the Gold Rush beginning in the 1850s and was settled by ranchers and cowboys. At one time the town boasted a ratio of twenty men to every one woman and the presence of more than three hundred bars and bordellos! Denver was no exemplar of style and sophistication.

Originally Denver became a small town in 1858 as a part of the Kansas Territory and was named after James W. Denver, the governor of the territory. Hungry speculators called "argonauts" were lured to the area after reports of the discovery of gold. That finding in turn brought with it an infusion of business developers and entrepreneurs who sought to make a profit from the demands of the growing population.

In describing the landscape of Denver during this time, travel writer Rose Kingsley said this: "It was as if the angels were carrying a city to a proper place and accidentally dropped it here."[6]

An early sign that Denver's citizens were entrepreneurial took place when the transcontinental railroad was completed in 1870. Originally, the railroad was set to bypass Denver, but a group of leaders in the town found the means to build a railroad that connected the city of Denver to Cheyenne, Wyoming, so Denver was assured of being linked to both the east and west coasts. In 1876 Colorado became the thirty-eighth state and Denver became its state capital in 1881.

At the same time transportation to Denver was improving, the silver boom that had begun soon after the Gold Rush and that had also wooed investors west began to wane. Those who had made millions in mining towns like Leadville and Central City were seeking lower ground in Denver. They brought with them their opulent lifestyles, and they built grand mansions that were much larger than the modest shacks they had left in the mountains. Mostly, they settled in and around Capitol Hill.

The move of these families caused an explosion of development. Laborers and domestic servants settled in the community to serve the demands of the wealthy families. Government, religious, and medical institutions were established.

Bankers and industrialists further aided the city's development, as did farmers, miners, and railroad workers from the outlying areas of the city. Dairies, flour mills, stockyards, and eventually sugar mills were opened for business to help feed a burgeoning community. A local flour mill hired Chase's father, Frank.

Opportunists and visionaries set to work to create a city of importance and stature that could compete with any other city in the country. In 1893, after Denver officials visited the World's Columbian Exposition in Chicago, the firm of New York's celebrated Central Park landscape designer Frederick Olmsted was hired as a consultant to plan the beautification of Denver. Streets were widened into boulevards, a park system was established, and the historic Red Rocks Amphitheatre was built.

Slowly but surely the city came together and gained a sense of identity, always with the intention of emulating the glamour more associated with New York and Europe.

Nothing could explain the city's desire for respectability better than the creation of a Denver High Society. That accomplishment was performed by Louise Sneed Hill, a member of one of the six families who, Chase was later to say, ran the city. The story goes that Mrs. Hill came from the South and a refined and elegant society milieu. When she met and married her husband, Crawford Hill, the son of a Colorado senator whose father had made fortunes during the silver boom, she settled down in Denver and concentrated on transferring her new hometown into a more exciting place to live. She decorated her mansion in rich brocades and silks, threw lavish parties to which she invited celebrities and royalty, and traveled extensively to New York and Europe, bringing back all the latest trends to introduce to the admiring locals.

In a similar fashion to that of New York doyenne Mrs. Cornelius Vanderbilt who had established "The 400," the number of people she could fit into her extravagant ballroom to attend star-studded events with guests like opera star Enrico Caruso, Mrs. Crawford Hill created the "Sacred Thirty-Six," the number of ladies that she could comfortably accommodate in her gilded dining room for an afternoon of cards.

Newspaper society editors regularly reported on and glamorized the balls and parties given by the Sacred Thirty-Six members. Mary Coyle Chase later became one of those reporters.

In addition to the Sacred Thirty-Six, Mrs. Hill also began to publish a *Blue Book Register* that listed all the people she considered to be the most influential and most entertaining individuals in town. They included millionaire residents, professionals who were moving the city forward, and a few literary and cultural leaders. The *Blue Book* continued to have a lasting influence on the city's population until 1994 when it finally stopped publication. The Chases were never among those listed as members.

Most famously the Sacred Thirty-Six was portrayed in *The Unsinkable Molly Brown* movie (1964) starring Debbie Reynolds. Like Mary Chase, Molly

Brown was an Irish immigrant whose family was new to America. Brown arrived in the 1800s and settled in the mining town of Leadville, Colorado. She married J. J. Brown, another poor immigrant who had become wealthy during the silver boom. When the Browns moved to Denver, Molly Brown was rejected from Mrs. Hill's inner circle until she became nationally famous for her courageous efforts to save people from drowning during the 1912 sinking of the ocean liner RMS *Titanic*.

Many of Chase's works delight in mocking the upper class. In *Harvey*, she satirizes the snobbish boasting of early New England *Mayflower* ship descendants by having Veta, in the opening scene, tell a society reporter that her mother, Marcella P. Dowd, the originator of the Wednesday Forum that she's hosting, was a pioneer cultural leader who came here by "ox-team." She describes in lofty terms what those attending the tea are wearing. "Rancho Rose," she explains, is the color of her daughter's dress, and Veta Simmons's aunt wears a fur even though it's summertime.

Mary Chase always thought of Denver as a cow town that missed many of the elements of a more refined approach to art and culture. Nevertheless, she resided in the city for all seventy-four of her years.

THE FAMILY

Each night over dinner, all the Coyles and McDonoughs would gather in the family dining room located behind the front parlor to have dinner. The wide-eyed Coyle children listened raptly as the uncles relayed all kinds of vivid gory Irish tales with great timing and in an Irish lilt. Chase and her brother Charlie were particularly enchanted by the stories of pookas, changelings, leprechauns, and banshees. They loved hearing stories about acts of evil in which eventually the villains came to see the good in life.[7]

It was after dinner, when Chase supposedly had retired for the evening, that she recalled sitting at the top of the stairs of her home as a constant deluge of her uncles' "greenhorn friends"[8] dropped by to visit and gather in the darkened first floor parlor alit with candles. Here they would drink whiskey, do some crow's nest dancing, talk about life, and debate politics. When she was older, Chase was amazed to learn that Oliver Cromwell (the controversial political leader of England, Scotland, and Ireland beginning in 1599) had been dead for hundreds of years. Explained Chase to an interviewer: "I thought he played pool at Dooley's at West Eighth Avenue and Santa Fe Drive" (down the street from their home).[9]

Over the distant sounds of the train whistles, she could hear the dialogue below:

"Well Joe, do you think you'll ever go back?"
"Not 'til they build a bridge back."[10]

A roar of laughter followed. Amid the comings and goings and drinking and singing of the visitors, the banter was repeated night after night.

In later years Chase credited her Irish heritage as a major influence on her writings. Indeed the ways of the Irish were an aspect of her overall view of life. She was always superstitious, loved seeking the pot of gold at the end of the rainbow, consistently championed the little guy, and never took life too seriously.

Chase's mother was a church-going Catholic who relied on her Celtic roots for her grounding. She felt that her mission in life was to always be generous and kind. Even when times were tough, she was inclined to give away food to those who had "a sorrow in the family."[11] She believed strongly in the supernatural and predicted the death of her father who lived in Ireland.

Above all, Chase's mother was a humanitarian. Once Chase and her mother were walking down an icy street in the midst of winter when they observed some boys throwing snowballs at an old woman walking with a cane. Mary Coyle cautioned her daughter, "Never be unkind or indifferent to a person others say is crazy. Often they have a deep wisdom. We pay them a great respect in the old country and we call them fairy people, and it could be, they are sometimes."[12]

Harvey's humane character reflects the words of Chase's mother about the need to respect the differences in people. Elwood P. Dowd, the companion of the imaginary six-foot, one-and-a-half-inch rabbit named Harvey, is a good man, gentle, full of humor, kind, but he isn't exactly of this world.

Chase's mother was a devout homemaker who took care of her husband, her children, and her brothers without a trace of resentment. She did all the chores relegated to traditional wives, and she saved every dollar that she could. A believer in beauty and art, she lovingly embroidered designs she had learned from the nuns of Londonderry in the old country on her daughter's underwear that she fashioned out of old flour sacks.

Seldom was Chase's mother successful in attempting to control her daughter's tomboy tendencies. A mischievous Mary regularly mounted her large shiny tricycle, sped around the neighborhood, and occasionally pelted a nearby neighbor's window with a rock.

Assimilating into a more middle-class neighborhood proved difficult for all the Coyle children, and this later became the subject for many of Chase's plays. Her characters were often in the middle of all kinds of tussles brought on by their daredevil antics. One particular incident completely ostracized the family and was the source of great humiliation. Chase's brother Charlie was shot by a policeman and arrested after he and his friends shook down a gumball machine. The day after the arrest took place, a story appeared in the Sunday newspapers. As she attended church with her mother, Chase could hear mothers of her friends telling their children not to speak to her. Charlie recovered from his injury and the policeman responsible was later dismissed for wrongdoing.[13] Still the rejection of the Coyles continued and proved to be painful for the entire family. The difficulty of fitting in became a common theme for many of Chase's stories and a likely reason she desired to stand out in a crowd. Charlie too felt the impact. He later ran away and, for a while, became a circus clown.

Another reason for the Chases' disenfranchisement was the times in which Chase was growing up. In the early 1900s there was strong resentment for the millions of new immigrants who had arrived in America and that included the Irish, Italians, Jews, African Americans, and Asians. This disapproval was reinforced by the rise in population of the white nationalist Ku Klux Klan organization that began to surface and continued to rise until 1924 when new anti-immigration laws were passed. Across the nation open hostilities against minorities were rampant and commonplace. It is unclear whether the Coyle children felt left out because they were Irish or because they were known to behave mischievously.

2

LI'L MARY

YOUNG AMERICA

Mary Agnes McDonough Coyle made her world stage debut in an America that was full of promise. After becoming president when William McKinley was assassinated in 1901, the ebullient Theodore Roosevelt promised a "Square Deal" for all. And that included one for Frank and Mary Coyle, Chase's Irish immigrant mother and her second-generation Irish father.

This era followed the preceding Gilded Age that had been named by Mark Twain to characterize a time of the creation of huge amounts of wealth. The new titans of industry, often referred to as the robber barons, had become millionaires in steel (Andrew Carnegie), shipping and railroads (Cornelius Vanderbilt), oil and gas (John D. Rockefeller), and banking (J.P. Morgan). Their wealth benefited the masses but heightened the disparity between the rich and the poor.

The change in administration did not alter the fact that America was experiencing rapid growth and modernization.

Major technological discoveries and inventions were occurring. Skyscrapers jutted through the clouds of major cities across the country. Bridges, subways, and railroads connected urban and rural America. Thomas Edison's discovery of the light bulb in 1898 lit up factories, streets, and homes. Henry Ford's Model T was invented but did not replace the horse and buggy throughout the town and country until 1913 when he created the first assembly line. Time-saving machines made life easier for the homemaker, the farmer, and the laborer.

The success of these new industries called for the addition of a larger workforce. To fill this need, beginning in the late 1800s, more than eight million immigrants arrived on America's shores from the British Isles, from the Mediterranean and Slavic regions of Europe, as well as from Asia. At the same time that new immigrants were coming to America, African Americans began a "Great Migration" from the south to the north where the job opportunities were better and they could escape the south's repressive Jim Crow laws.

Further stimulating the country to think in new ways were the introduction of Sigmund Freud's revelation of psychoanalysis in 1898 and Albert Einstein's discovery of the Theory of Relativity in 1905.

On the domestic front, incidents of all kinds threatened a peaceful life. The Ku Klux Klan committed violent acts against the new immigrants and rose to power throughout the early twentieth century. Workers protested unfair labor practices. Politicians looked for loopholes to get ahead. Bank robbers increased in number. Natural disasters like dust storms and floods devastated the plains.

Internationally, President Roosevelt initiated the opening of the Panama Canal to encourage trade; President William Howard Taft advocated an "Open Door" policy that welcomed immigrants to American shores; and Woodrow Wilson, after he became president in 1913, reversed his campaign pledge to stay out of World War I and sent American soldiers to Europe in 1917 until the war ended in 1918. Mary Coyle's brother Frank was a member of the armed forces.

Under these three presidents, controversies of immigration, labor disputes, currency issues, economic controls, and anti-trust concerns resulted in four new constitutional amendments. In 1913 the sixteenth amendment established a federal income tax; the seventeenth amendment allowed citizens to directly elect senators; the eighteenth amendment prohibited the sale and production of liquor and passed in 1918; and the nineteenth amendment gave women the right to vote in 1920.

Like their fellow countrymen, Chase's parents connected to the rest of the world with all of the means of transportation and communication available to them: streetcars in 1904; the more than eight thousand newspapers that circulated throughout the country; numerous magazines and catalogues; and beginning in 1910, the newsreels that were featured at local movie houses. They talked on an expanding network of telephone lines, and they wrote and received mail by an accelerated postal service. Radio, television, talking movies, and airplanes would be introduced to the masses in the not too distant future.

To pass their growing leisure time, Americans attended sporting events like baseball games and boxing matches; enjoyed traveling minstrel shows, circuses, vaudeville, and touring theater productions; and stepped into nickelodeons in storefront theaters to view seven- or eight-minute-long silent movie pictures and soon after into movie palaces to watch longer versions starring popular actors like Charlie Chaplin and native Denverite Douglas Fairbanks, Sr. They attended military concerts hosted by John Philip Sousa and listened to ragtime music they could play on Thomas Edison's newly invented phonograph.

The recently arrived Coyles and McDonoughs faced this "New World" with optimism, humor, and joy. They were determined to be an integral part of these wondrous times. So would the next generation to come, including Mary Coyle.

SCHOOL DAYS

At the age of five, Mary began her education at Fairmont School, a five-room Denver public school located a few blocks from where the Coyle family lived. Chase's principal watched a fidgety young lady who had as much difficulty concentrating in the classroom as she had getting along on the playground. In Chase's plays and books, conflicts with her peers are common themes reminiscent of her past. The gang on the other side of the tracks in her play *Mrs. McThing* is always sparring, and in *The Dog Sitters*, best friends Christine and Beverly are fond of exchanging insults with one another. "Brat," says Christine. "Chicken," responds Beverly.[1]

After Fairmont Elementary, Mary moved on to West High School. Among the attendees of the school who preceded her were Paul Whiteman and screenwriter Gene Fowler. The school was a typical public school of the day. Pictures of football teams, homecoming celebrations, and student government officers all appear in Chase's high school yearbook. Chase's interests were in debate, public speaking, and singing, rather than cheerleading, writing for the class newspaper, or running for prom queen. Chase is remembered by one of her classmates as "a young lady who stood sedately and proudly in a navy blue accordion dress topped by a blue and white collar and knotted tie. Her pointed shoes were covered by buttoned leggings."[2]

Chase was bright and learned quickly. She continued her outsider status and insubordinate manner and graduated from West in three years at the age of fifteen.

3

THE LURE OF THE THEATER

A DAY AT THE DENHAM

On a lovely spring day in the year 1918, eleven-year-old Mary Coyle was having a case of spring fever. In her typical defiant manner, she made a decision to skip her school classes and head to downtown Denver.

Instead of taking the streetcar near her modest middle-class home, to save money she walked several blocks north to Theatre Row, known by locals as "The Great White Way."

She was dressed in her older sister's hand-me-down frocks that, when the wind blew, revealed cotton underwear with the words "Pride of the Rockies" emblazoned on them (the emblem of the Hungarian Flour Mill where her father worked). As she confidently walked, her dark curly hair bounced in step. She was feeling liberated from the regular playground spats in which she was frequently involved and from the constant calls that she got to the principal's office for being a troublemaker. She had been spending a lot of time reading books since she turned eight and now she was ready to expand her interests and pursue the theater.

Most of the theaters were located on Curtis Street, but there were also a number of theaters on the side streets as well. On nearby California Street Mary Coyle was attracted to a crowd that had gathered in front of the six-story Denham Theatre. The marquee announced the fare: "The Wilkes Players Company Presents Shakespeare's *Macbeth*."*

---

*Accounts by both Mary and her early biographers offer different versions of her first theater-going experience. Instead of *Macbeth*, the first play might have been *Hamlet* or *Merchant of Venice*, and the theater could have been the Orpheum or the Broadway rather than the Denham.

Mary was intrigued. She paid a quarter for her ticket, entered the lobby lavishly decorated with sparkling chandeliers and royal blue and gold velvet drapes, and climbed the stairs to the top balcony of the theater where she took her seat.

The lights dimmed, the audience hushed, and the curtains parted on the scene of a desert. Amid the sound of thunder and lightning, three witches appeared on the set and the play began:

> First Witch: When shall we three meet again?
> In thunder, in lighting, or in rain?
> Second Witch: When the hurlyburly's done,
> When the battle's lost and won.
> Third Witch: That will ere the set of sun.[1]

From that wondrous moment, there was no doubt for Mary Coyle. She was going to be a playwright.

Many more days would follow when she would opt to skip school and attend a production. She would view melodramas, Shakespearean comedies and tragedies, vaudeville companies, and the most popular Broadway theater fare of the time, and she would love them all. The Great White Way lured her again and again. She was enchanted and star struck. She knew right away that she didn't want to act, direct, design sets, or make costumes; she just wanted to write plays, and, just like all the ones she continued to view once she discovered the magic of the theater, to see them produced on the stage.

THE GREAT WHITE WAY

Denver's first theater production took place in 1859, the same year that Denver became a city. In the beginning the productions were mostly melodramas and were often presented on the second story above the local bar. When the families of silver barons lived in the mountain towns of Central City and Leadville, massive opera houses had been built to bring all of the best of eastern entertainment to the west, and when those families moved to Denver, they brought with them a rich tradition of embracing the theater. As a result many theaters were built to bring a wide array of entertainment to Denver dwellers.

Beginning in the late 1800s, theater developers began to construct elaborate edifices with names like Isis, Orpheum, and Broadway. The bill of fare included dramatic presentations or vaudeville productions. To draw people into their venues, producers often provided "leads" before the main attraction such as live animal shows and circus acts. Marquees were hoisted above the buildings to announce the featured guests. Theaters were paneled with rich woods and enhanced with velvet and marble.

The most extravagant of these theaters, the Tabor Grand Opera House, was built in 1881. The opening was a two-week festival of the Grand English Opera

Company and featured soprano Emma Abbott who was guaranteed twenty thousand dollars for her appearance as well as three thousand dollars for her rail transportation. Silver king Horace Tabor had commissioned the building and hired architect Willoughby Edbrooke to "tour the great opera houses of the day to collect ideas."[2] That included opera houses in London and Paris. "The Tabor was luxurious with Belgian carpets, French tapestries, Japanese cherry wood, Honduras mahogany, and marble floors. Considered large for the day, it seated 1,550."[3]

Three years before Chase was born, in 1904 Robert Speer became mayor of Denver and began a public relations campaign to bring more tourists and settlers to Denver. He touted the downtown theater district and asked theater owners to light up their theater facades with thousands of lights to replicate the wonder of New York's Coney Island Park that was called the Great White Way. To further showcase the more than sixty-six theaters of various persuasions that were located on and near Curtis Street, Speer spent millions of dollars on a glossy pamphlet showcasing the district. Soon Denver boasted of its own Great White Way.

The theaters offered a variety of entertainment including melodramas and burlesque and vaudeville shows. Concerts featured popular entertainers of the day like Georgie Jessel, the Gumm Sisters (one of whom would change her name to Judy Garland), the Marx Brothers, and Paul Whiteman's band. Serious legitimate theater also found its way to the strip with versions of the most popular current productions that were taking place on Broadway. Chase's first theater attendance at a production of *Macbeth* was performed by one of several resident stock companies.

To make the offer even more enticing, in the 1920s it was not uncommon for the theaters to have side rooms for dice games and gambling, speakeasies, and pool halls.

THE LIBRARY AND THE THEATER

At an early age Chase started paying visits to her school library. When Andrew Carnegie, as part of a national plan, funded the Byers Library that was built in her neighborhood in 1917, it allowed Chase even more opportunities for her curious mind to seek out all kinds of stories and tales.

Chase credits the origins of her thirst for reading good literature to the time when she was eight years old and the school librarian gave her a copy of Charles Dickens's *A Tale of Two Cities*. Much later in life, she told a Canadian Broadcasting interviewer that when she was cleaning out her house, she found the book with a note in the flyleaf: "My name is Mary Coyle and I have just read this book. Don't you think I'm smart?"[4] To the interviewer she then commented: "Eight years old! What a brat!"[5]

"I read everything,"[6] she professed. Though history shows that Americans during this time were reading *Alice in Wonderland*, the *Wizard of Oz*, *Tarzan* stories, and novels by Willa Cather, Chase claims to have been most interested in Greek mythology. She also found the work of Thomas DeQuincey, a popular Catholic English writer who wrote about the supernatural, to be particularly intriguing. At the beginning she was drawn to the name DeQuincey, but once she began to read his work Chase was fascinated by his taste for the underworld that was full of mysterious animals and objects and events.

Throughout her life Chase remained a passionate and eclectic reader on a wide range of topics from the classics to the contemporary.

Her interest in books expanded to the theater when her Uncle Jamie gave her a gift of a dollar and she decided to skip school and explore downtown Denver. From the time that she saw her first play, whether it was *Macbeth* or *Hamlet* or *As You Like It*, Chase began a lifelong love affair with the theater.

She returned over and over again to the Curtis Street theater district. Every extra quarter was spent on an afternoon at the theater. She viewed tragedies, comedies, farces, and melodramas with titles such as *Turn to the Right*, *Vagabond King*, *School for Scandal*, and *Bird of Paradise*.

From the moment she discovered the theater, her raucous behavior began to subside. She continued to stir up trouble throughout her life, but the theater helped to tame her devilish tendencies.

One day, while visiting the library, Chase discovered a book called *Playmaking: A Manual of Craftsmanship*, written by William Archer. The book was written in 1911 and continues to be a mainstay among works on the craft of playwriting. In addition to introducing Mary to the elements of the play, such as character, plot, exposition, theme, crisis, and climax, it also offered an overall belief that, after a certain amount of study, one must rely on one's own instincts to complete the work.

> There are no rules for writing a play. It is easy, indeed, to lay down negative recommendations—to instruct the beginner how *not* to do it. But most of these "don'ts" are rather obvious; and those which are not obvious are apt to be questionable. It is certain, for instance, that if you want your play to be acted, anywhere else than in China, you must not plan it in sixteen acts of an hour apiece.[7]

4

LEAVING THE NEST

As gifted as Mary Coyle was in brainpower, she was also growing up and becoming a very attractive young woman. She had porcelain skin, wide grey eyes, dark curly hair flecked with hints of red, and beautiful legs. The combination of brains and beauty were definite assets when it came to pursuing her dreams.

CLASSICAL COLLEGE

In 1922, Mary Coyle, fifteen years old and a recent high school graduate, enrolled at the University of Denver and began to study the classics. Her parents had saved enough money to send their child prodigy to pursue higher learning.

Originally founded in 1864 as the Colorado Seminary by John Evans, a territorial governor, the college had begun to allow the enrollment of women in 1880. The school was privately endowed. It was founded as a city school for all to attend, but it had a reputation for being somewhat exclusive. According to the daughter of a friend of Bob and Mary Chase's, the University of Denver was nicknamed "Tramway U" because many of the children of the executives from the Denver streetcar company were enrolled at the school.[1] Chase did not have the lineage or the wealth that many of her fellow students possessed. Nevertheless, she was accepted to study at the university. Rather than live on campus, she commuted from her nearby neighborhood.

The reason that she decided to study the classics was based on her desire to learn English grammar. "We were told then that that was the best way to learn it."[2]

It's quite possible that her interest in the classics had more to do with her desire to become respected. The study of the Greek and Roman classics was considered to be the cornerstone of a typical elite education. Chase was a talented mimic and after taking these courses, she used her new knowledge to assume the airs of a more refined nature to impress her peers. When she later became a reporter at the *Rocky Mountain News*, she often was known to take time out to rattle off monologues in Greek and Latin.

Regardless of her intentions, Chase immersed herself in learning Greek and Latin and in reading the works of scholars who were writing during those ancient times.

She especially singled out her interest in *Anabasis*, a classic text by the Greek writer Xenophon (431–355 BC) that recounts the expedition of the Persian prince Cyrus the Younger and his conflict with his brother, King Artaxerxes II, and that most likely helped to inspire Chase to write stories that revolved around family relationships.

The literature of this ancient time is full of all kinds of devious plots that demonstrate human frailty: evil wives like Medea, longing poets like Sappho, and adventurers like Odysseus. They laid the groundwork for Chase's future ventures into the playwriting world.

Chase later cited three specific courses at the University of Denver as being particularly influential: a course on the Renaissance and medieval history, one that she took at the religious college next door to the university, and one on journalism. Each of these courses steered her future beliefs and the subject matter she chose to put into her plays and books.

Taking a course in medieval and Renaissance history was notably influential in leading Chase to a more spiritual approach to religion. In contrast to her upbringing and to her mother's strong Catholic influence, Chase went through several evolutions before settling on a more secular kind of attitude toward the church. Throughout her life she consistently read the Bible, prayed in her closet when she felt the need, and eventually found comfort from membership at a Christian Scientist church rather than from the Catholic Church in which she was raised.

After two years at the University of Denver, Chase finally came to believe it was time to surface and meet up with the living. Though she did not return for her junior year, in 1947 the University of Denver conferred an honorary degree on Mary Coyle Chase after she won the Pulitzer Prize for *Harvey*.

A NEWS BREAK

In the summer of 1924, dressed in a lacy black dress and wearing a floppy black hat, Chase presented herself to William C. Shankin, the managing editor of the *Rocky Mountain News*, one of the city's two major newspapers. Though it's not clear by those who worked for the paper at the time whether it was her good looks or her audacity that got her hired at the age of seventeen, Chase nevertheless was hired. Her salary was an amount of money that paid for her carfare.

Chase said she wanted to be a street reporter so she could "study people, meet life and . . . put (them) into plays like all the ones she had seen growing up."[3] She wanted to see how people reacted under stress, how they spoke "in times of crisis."[4] She believed the best way to learn was to work for a newspaper.

"I really wanted to get in the swing of things," she said, "and I wanted news-paper experience because I wanted to hear the rhythm of speech from people in these dramatic situations of life."[5]

It's not clear if she had met anyone along the way that might have influenced her desire to join the newspaper world.

A possible influence might have been a neighbor, Alice Polk Hill, a future Colorado Poet Laureate and a member of the Denver Women's Press Club. Chase did briefly join the organization in 1925. The Denver Women's Press Club had begun in 1898 and had already attracted a number of female journalists, many of them who were "sob sisters," female reporters who covered stories about lost and found dogs, high-profile divorces, and society balls.

After *Harvey* became a success, Chase was the first living person to become a lifetime honorary member of the club.

One of the earliest of the sob sisters was Polly Pry, the controversial reporter who worked for the *Denver Post* in the late nineteenth and early twentieth centu-ries and was best known for her interview with the cannibalist Alferd Packer. An-other well-known early female reporter was Nellie Bly, who was one of the first women to be recognized for her investigative reporting and worked in New York.

It was too soon for Chase to have been influenced by the movies that began in the early 1940s when movie stars popularized the image of the tough female re-porter in offerings like *His Girl Friday* (1940) starring Rosalind Russell and Cary Grant and *Woman of the Year* (1942) with Katharine Hepburn and Spencer Tracy.

Literary Mary Coyle was familiar with the female journalists of the day who were making contributions to popular newspapers and magazines in Denver and around the country. Later she explained to an interviewer that working in "the newspaper biz was a very glamorous job."[6]

There was a certain segment of the female population both nationally and lo-cally who frequented the world of journalism at the time Chase entered the throes. According to journalism professor Donna Born:

> The 1920s offered unprecedented opportunity to women journalists because of the popularity of magazines and the insatiable public demand for news, especially the zany, the sensational, the emotional, and the scandalous.[7]

When Chase began her journalism career, female journalists made up 24 percent of the profession. Most of these journalists were not household names and were scattered throughout the country, and most of them served in the role of society columnists and "sob sisters."

NO SORORITY FOR MARY

After her internship, Chase returned to college, but this time she decided to attend the University of Colorado in Boulder. Founded in 1877, the imposing campus was located at the foothills of the Rocky Mountains. Chase felt a sense of freedom to be away from the confines of the neighborhood where everybody knew her name.

In a short amount of time the exhilaration she initially felt was replaced by dejection.

Once she had arrived on campus, Chase decided to go through rush week and try to join a sorority. Fraternities and sororities had been on campus at colleges across the country since the middle of the nineteenth century. They were intended to create social bonds among its members. The desire to become part of a group was an attempt on Chase's part to break down barriers and lose the notion of being an outsider.

After attending all the recruitment parties, not one invitation to become a sorority girl was offered to her. Chase was devastated.

One of Chase's first plays that followed her retirement from working for the *News* was *Chi House*, and it concerned her rejection from a sorority. It made its debut at the University of Denver Civic Theatre as *Sorority House* and then became a movie by the same name in 1939.

Reflecting about this time later in life, Chase told an interviewer that when she was attending the sorority party events, she had shabby clothes and did not have the money or the status required for an ultimate invitation.[8]

At the end of her junior year, Mary Coyle left college for good. Her feelings were reflected in the lines she wrote for *Sorority House* where her character does not want to stay and be with the outsiders that she calls "Barbarians." "Stay and go to Barbarian dances? No thanks—besides I've had quite an education already."[9]

Her sights became set on a journalism career.

5

THE RAGING REPORTER

Chase left the university world for good in 1925. She'd had enough of the theory of living. Now it was time to participate in the practice of living. It was her hope that this would occur by becoming a permanent member of the *Rocky Mountain News* staff, but it took a while before this happened. As was typical, Chase pursued her goal with a vengeance.

Each morning of the week she left her home on West Fourth Avenue dressed in her formal attire of black dress, pearls, and high heels, a style that became her trademark. She felt that if she looked important, people would be more willing to share their stories with her.

Setting her sights on hospitals and jails, Chase armed herself with her old clothes that she offered to the occupants in exchange for their personal accounts that she then submitted to the newspapers for them to purchase and publish.

One day she visited an elderly man who was living out his last days in the corner of a rancid jail cell. As Chase watched him struggle, she wrestled with the question of how to lead a life of meaning for herself and to share with others. She settled on an idea that would remain a consistent guidepost for her. Rather than following a religious path, she would choose a spiritual one that was governed by a pursuit of love, laughter, and beauty.[1]

Months after leaving college and looking for stories about life, she was finally hired by the *News* as a society columnist for fifteen dollars a week.

At last Chase had become a part of the glamorous newspaper world of the Roaring Twenties that she had dreamed of joining.

THE ROARING TWENTIES

America in the 1920s was all about derring-do. The painful memories of the atrocities of World War I were placed on hold. There was a need to break out, make waves, and kick up one's heels.

Helped along by the passing of the eighteenth amendment prohibiting the sale and production of alcohol, underground mayhem in the form of speakeasies, bootleggers, and gangsters was commonplace.

The news of the day ranged from national stories like corruption in the Harding administration to the Scopes Monkey Trial of 1925 to the first transoceanic flight of Charles Lindbergh in 1927.

On the international front, the ensuing rise of fascism was brewing but not yet making headlines.

The passage of the nineteenth amendment in 1920 gave women the long-sought-after right to vote. (Colorado was one of the first states to pass such a law in 1893.) In addition, women felt a sense of liberation that was helped along by Planned Parenthood founder Margaret Sanger's introduction in 1921 to birth control and by the discovery of all kinds of time-saving domestic devices like the washing machine, the refrigerator, and the vacuum cleaner.

John Lewis, a *Rocky Mountain News* reporter at the time who later become city editor and then assistant managing editor, recalled the climate of the Roaring Twenties that made it so inviting for journalists: "It was a wonderful, fearful, rowdy time and place for newspapering," he writes, "especially for those of us who were just breaking in."[2]

Chase joined her female peers and took on the guise of the trendy flapper style. She bobbed her hair, shortened her skirts, and painted her lips red. In between running around town for her reporting job, she unabashedly drank, smoked, and played. She was the epitome of what Dorothy Parker, acclaimed poet and wit of the time, said about flappers: "They were not what grandma used to be."[3]

The general population was enjoying the American pastimes of the day: dancing to the Charleston and watching silent screen movies until talking movies debuted in 1927. Among the first to be shown was the sensational hit *The Jazz Singer* featuring popular singer Al Jolson. There were exciting boxing matches between Gene Tunney and Coloradoan Jack Dempsey and rousing baseball games with New York Yankees players Babe Ruth and Lou Gehrig. Folks were listening to songs by George Gershwin and Duke Ellington, reading books by F. Scott Fitzgerald and Ernest Hemingway, and, if they were lucky enough to visit New York, seeing Broadway plays by Eugene O'Neill and Clifford Odets or, like Chase, read about them in *Variety*.

THE DENVER NEWSPAPER WORLD

At the time Chase was hired by the *Rocky Mountain News*, there were five Denver newspapers. The *Rocky Mountain News* was the oldest. It had begun on April 23, 1859, only months after Denver had become a city and in response to the discovery of gold nearby. The founder, William Byers, arrived from Kansas with a printing press twenty minutes before another fellow journalist and began the *Rocky Mountain News*. He bought out his competitor the next day for flour and bacon. Many attempts by others to publish the news followed. The *News*'s major competition was the *Denver Post*, which began in 1895 when two colorful fellows, Harry Tammen, a local bartender and owner of a curio shop, and Frederick Bonfils, a struggling businessman from Kansas City, decided to challenge the *Rocky Mountain News*. Tammen and Bonfils prided themselves on reporting gossip, and their sensational yellow journalism attracted advertisers who paid large sums to be noticed in their papers. Thus began a fierce rivalry between the two papers, with reporters and editors scrambling to beat out the other for the top stories of the day.

Violence, crime, murder, and suicide were daily occurrences, and reporters were intent on making sure a human tragedy never slipped by without notice. As in other cities throughout the country, Denver had its share of noteworthy events: the robbery of the Denver Mint in 1922, the national and local exposé of the Teapot Dome Scandal that involved secret payoffs for access to government oil reserves, the membership of Mayor Ben Stapleton in the Ku Klux Klan, and the routing out of payoffs to police by those seeking to assure the existence of underground crime. There was coverage of mass attendance at revivals by Aimee Semple McPherson and other faith healers, and of a Tramway streetcar strike in which several onlookers were killed. Many incidents of graft and financial incompetence foreshadowed the coming Great Depression of 1929.

The Denver news scene was an incubator for many writers who became well known on the national scene. Poet Eugene Field, best known for his classic children's poem, "Wynken, Blynken, and Nod," arrived in Denver from Kansas City in 1881 and worked for the then *Denver Tribune*. An iconoclast by nature, he was a bit too brassy for the more conservative Denver community. He blatantly criticized many of the most revered leaders in the city. He was a big prankster who is still best known for the time he dressed up as the touring actor and playwright Oscar Wilde and made an appearance at an event where Wilde was supposed to be speaking.

Dalton Trumbo, the future screenwriter who was later blacklisted by the House Un-American Activities Committee and is best known for writing blockbuster screenplays including *Spartacus* and *Exodus*, also practiced journalism for a while in Colorado, in nearby Grand Junction and in Boulder where he attended the University of Colorado at the same time that Mary Coyle was in attendance. In 1938 Dalton Trumbo and Chase collaborated on Chase's first screenplay, *Sorority House*.

Another early Denver reporter who achieved national fame was Damon Runyon whose literary portraits of underground characters became the inspiration for the iconic musical *Guys and Dolls*. From 1900 to 1910 he worked first for the *Denver Post* and then for the *Rocky Mountain News*. On his beat he covered local politics and sports. Eventually he moved on to New York.

Other journalists and authors who had connections to Denver during the early twentieth century included Katherine Anne Porter, who went on to write the popular novel *Ship of Fools* and who worked for the *Rocky Mountain News* in 1918 as a society reporter. Gene Fowler, another local writer, became a Hollywood screenwriter and is best known for his controversial 1914 interview with Buffalo Bill Cody in which Cody's many extramarital affairs were revealed. Famed broadcaster Lowell Thomas grew up in nearby Cripple Creek, Colorado, and wrote for the *Victor Record* and then went on to attend the University of Denver in 1912. Nebraska's Willa Cather did research at the Denver Public Library in 1914 for her book, *Death Comes to the Archbishop*.

Future Colorado poet laureate Thomas Ferril originally wrote for several local newspapers before becoming a full-time publicist for The Great Western Sugar Company, a position he held for the remainder of his life. In his free time he wrote poems that were published in national and local publications. He and his wife, Helen, often entertained visiting literary stars of the day like Robert Frost, Carl Sandburg, and Dorothy Parker in their East Denver home.

Almost all of these distinctive writers of the 1920s who spent some time in Denver moved on to higher profile positions in New York, Los Angeles, or Chicago. The two that remained in Denver were Thomas Ferril and Mary Coyle Chase.

AUDACIOUS MARY

Like most women of the times, Mary began her journalism career as a society reporter.

"The Davis Whitney Nuptial" by Mary Coyle

The bride wore a lovely gown, an imported French model of white satin covered with an embroidery of seed pearls, rhinestones and crystals. The gown was fashioned after the bouffant mode with a full skirt and snug bodice, and made without sleeves.[4]

It did not take long for Mary to branch out to other less frequented beats for women. Cartoonist Charlie Wunder and Mary became the duo of Li'l Mary and Charlie, and together wrote entertaining social commentary such as this one about "collitch."

"Member of Grabba Bolla Soupa Greets Cartoonist as Blood Brother in Fraternity"

Charlie: "Mary, do higher skirts and higher learning go hand in hand?"

Mary: "We both just stood and stared at a bunch of bozoes roaming acrost the campus, all decked out in big wide trousers, red and green sweaters and bow ties that looked like miniature windmills."[5]

Another year later Mary wrote her own humorous column. Mary's photo precedes the article. She takes a vamp pose and wears a cloche hat on her head and a scarf that swoops around her neck.

"Whisperer's Campaign Rejected by Both Parties"

When I went to school the teacher used to get right up before the class and say "Where there's whispering to be done, I can always depend on Mary to do it." It's always been a point of pride with me that I never say anything to a person's face that I can say behind their back.[6]

She begins by saying she is hoping that her whispering will get her a job. First she tries the Republican candidate:

I know something about Hoover that's not so good. A friend of mine heard it from a friend of his who knew a Pullman porter that rode the same train as he did once. I leaned over and whispered, "Hoover wears a corset—sniff that snuff, willya?"[7]

The Republican rejects her whisper so then she goes to the Democrat:

You see, my brother-in-law's cousin married a girl whose sister used to live next door to Al Smith in New York City. She told her sister who told her cousin and her cousin told my brother-in-law and he told me that absolutely beyond a doubt, Al Smith sleeps in his underwear. Let's whisper that around.[8]

At the end of her tale neither party accepts the whisperer's news tips, and sadly Mary Coyle is forced to give her allegiance to the third party. Mary's imagination was in full swing.

None of her assignments satisfied Chase's desire to cover real life in the 1920s. She finally convinced her editor Eddie Day that he needed her to search after the real stories of the day. Accompanied by Harry Rhoads, the leading photographer of the *News* who had already taken many memorable photos in his twenty-year career, Chase rode in Rhoads's shiny two-cylinder Maxwell automobile and covered a full day's worth of events, often starting at the police court, then moving on to a murder trial, then to an evening soiree at Mrs. Hill's, and ending up in the late evening at a reported shooting.

"Mary," Rhoads said, "was the most beautiful reporter I ever met."[9]

Chase loved the reporter's life and she did it well, if not conventionally. She was not known for keeping regular hours but when she showed up with her copy, all was forgiven.

It was common among reporters of the day to steal photographs to print, and Chase specialized in this art. One time a famous divorce was taking place in town and her editor asked her to get a photo of the male socialite being sued by his wife. Nobody was able to find a photo. Then Chase remembered that there was a photo of the gentleman in his tennis clothes hanging on the wall of the Denver

Country Club. She arrived at the club, sauntered in, found her way to the corridor where the photo was hanging, nonchalantly removed the photo, raced out the door of the Country Club, hailed a passing truck, and ordered him to take her immediately to the downtown *Rocky Mountain News* headquarters. Soon after her acquisition the irate manager of the country club called up her editor who had already received the photo. It was returned in short order but not before it was copied for publication.

Once Chase offered to be a stunt girl, a common activity of the times in which a female reporter took a truth serum administered by the police to prove that a story was accurate. When she developed an infection after taking the serum, her editor became dismayed and thus ended Chase's venture into the world of stunt girls.

Chase's resilience reached its peak when she dressed as a man to be present at the opening of the Moffat Tunnel underneath the Continental Divide. Because women were not allowed to report on the construction of the dangerous site, Chase dressed herself in men's overalls and tucked up her hair in a bun under a cap before appearing at the meeting of the east and west bores. For the final drilling Jack Foster, a fellow *News* reporter, scrambled over the debris from the east and met Chase as she arrived from the west. Foster grabbed her and kissed her, and then dashed to the tunnel entrance and a telephone to get the scoop.

Denver was known at the time for its boxing matches at the local Denver Athletic Club where the most well-known boxers of the day often appeared. Again Chase broke the barrier and became the first female reporter to cover a match. The event turned particularly gory. Blood spilled all over the floor and she fainted but not for long. In an instant she revived and continued to cover the story.

On another occasion, Chase was covering a murder trial and she received a call from her father that their house was on fire. "Let me finish my story first,"[10] she replied. Afterwards she felt badly that she had lost a new dress she had just purchased. Her publishers bought her a replacement.

Regardless of the task, Chase remained steady, calm, and emotionless. After the engines went out on a plane in which she was riding with an associate of Charles Lindbergh's, she responded to the pilot in her usual nonplussed manner: "Now we can talk."[11]

In between the demands of covering the beat, she was known to hike herself onto a desk and recite poetry in Latin or join the guys for a few shots of whiskey. Her good looks were always on display. An Indian chief who had come to the office for an interview about the Old West once became distracted when he eyed the "blue dress squaw"[12] (Mary Coyle) working at the typewriter across the room. He asked the interviewer (Chase's boss) if he could strike a bargain in blankets for the squaw. The editors had to tell the chief she was not for sale.

THE CHRISTMAS DEMISE

The crowning moment that ultimately led to Chase's demise was a practical joke she played at Christmas on Eddie Day, the editor of the *Evening News*. Day was a morose type who was often described as "humorless."[13]

The *News* had sent holiday gift baskets to the indigent in an effort to engender goodwill. Mary Coyle called up Eddie and disguised her voice in an Irish brogue.

"There wasn't no turkey like your paper said. There was nothing but one measly sausage and some wormy apples," she complained. Then she went on: "It's a crying shame that anyone in the name of Christian charity would give poor children rotten apples."[14] Other reporters looked on as Eddie Day became apoplectic when he couldn't stop her tirade. Finally Chase hung up but then called back ten minutes later to continue complaining. Day stopped answering the phone. When he learned that Chase was the source of the Christmas basket prank, he fired her. Though he finally forgave her and rehired her, she was relegated to society reporting from that point on, most likely as punishment for playing a trick.

The Christmas incident signified the fateful downturn of Chase's reporting career. Her firing came in 1931, three years after Mary Coyle married fellow reporter Robert Chase and was getting ready to settle down and start a family.

The news job gave Chase what she wanted. "I studied how Mrs. Hill greeted guests in her mansion, the tight composure on the faces of the defendants in murder trials, and the way District Attorney Philip S. Van Cise walked like a Shakespearean Actor."[15]

She achieved her goal of attaining a window on real life. It was time to move on and begin to tell her stories.

6

SHE MEETS HER MAN

In 1926, the *Rocky Mountain News* acquired the *Denver Times*, and *Times* reporter Robert Lamont Chase became part of the *News* staff. Soon after he joined the paper he met Mary Coyle. It was the beginning of a lifetime relationship.

THE SOLID MAN

Robert Chase had started his career in 1922 after he happened to be in downtown Denver during the notorious Denver Mint robbery. He had only recently graduated from high school, but watching the excitement of the robbery unfold convinced him that he wanted to be in the front row and to report on the events of the day.

He applied at the *Denver Times*. The *Denver Times* had begun in 1906 and had become a spokesman for labor and progressives. It was described as "the only one with spunk enuf to expose the KKK when it began to run in the mid-twenties."[1]

From the beginning Chase was devoted to his profession whatever the job would be. Legend has it that at one point he substituted for a lovelorn columnist.

Robert Chase came from a comfortable background and was a dutiful son. He became a solid and devoted husband, father, and grandfather as well. By the time his career ended at the *Rocky Mountain News*, he had risen to the top position of associate editor. In his forty-seven years at the *News*, he covered many of the major news events of the times including the rise and fall of the Ku Klux Klan and the Teapot Dome scandal.

Colleagues remember Robert Chase as a "newspaperman's newspaperman" who uttered "devastating, entirely unprofane monosyllables" and "came by the palm honestly by way of a thorough knowledge of his city." He had a "faculty for keeping his head when everyone else (was) pacing the ceiling."[2] Added Clyde Davis, a contemporary reporter who later became a novelist, (he was) "a solid character."[3] Robert Chase's son Jerry described his father as "practical."[4]

Robert Chase's upbringing was much more refined than his future wife's. He was born in 1905 in Sutherland, Nebraska, to Albert Lamont Chase, a lawyer-teacher, and Clara Coates. He was the oldest of three boys. The Chase ancestors were whalers from Maine, and it was alleged that Chase's father was related to Margaret Chase Smith, the first woman in the United States ever to be elected a senator.

Robert Chase was a teenager when the Chase family moved to Lincoln, Nebraska. In 1920 the family moved again, this time to Denver where he finished his high school years at the highly regarded East High School. Word has it that during his high school years, he applied to be on the school newspaper and was rejected.[5]

Robert Chase joined the *Denver Times* in 1922 and worked there for four years before deciding he wanted to go to college. He chose to attend Notre Dame located in South Bend, Indiana. While attending school, he worked at the *South Bend News Times*.

When his father died, he returned to Denver to help take care of his mother and began working once more for the *Denver Times*. Soon after his return, the *Denver Times* became part of the *Rocky Mountain News*.

THE LURE

Robert Chase had dark penetrating eyes and a thick shock of black hair, and he stood well over six feet. His demeanor was quiet and gentle in manner and bore a resemblance to his wife's later description of Elwood P. Dowd. Unlike Elwood, he preferred to be a part of the real world.

Mary Coyle, however, was brash, outspoken, and aggressive. She also knew what she wanted and worked very hard to get it. That applied to her future spouse, Robert Chase.

Though their assignments were quite different, Mary and Bob's desks at the *News* were in proximity to one another. From his position in the newsroom he could see Mary chatting with colleagues while he, the industrious Robert Chase, sat at his desk in the corner working on copy.

From the moment Chase set eyes on her future husband, she knew he was the one. With the assistance of Jenette Letts, a fellow reporter and a friend, she devised a plan to lure "Mr. Right," the reserved Robert Chase. Jenette lent Chase a car and then each day as Bob was leaving work, she offered Bob a ride home. The plot worked, and it wasn't long before they were a couple.

THE KNOT

There is a persistent legend that Bob Chase and Mary Coyle were married June 6, 1928, during their lunch hour while they were waiting for a courtroom jury to return with its verdict. The truth is that they were married on that same Friday but in the evening after work at the First Church of Divine Science, a church that served the exclusive Capitol Hill community where many of the women members were faith healers. In attendance for Mary Coyle were two reporter friends of hers and her father, Frank Coyle. Bob Chase's brothers were also in attendance. His brother Wendell served as best man. Said the paper, "After a short honeymoon, they will return to their jobs at the paper."[6]

For the first years of their marriage the Chases lived with Mary's father Frank in her childhood home at 532 West Fourth Avenue. One reason Bob and Mary took up residence with Frank Coyle might have been to keep him company. Mary's mother and four uncles had already passed away. Because neither of the Chases had generous incomes, another reason might have been to save money.

Seven years later, after the birth of their second son, they finally moved into a house of their own. Though Mary asked her father to move with them, he refused. The house, he explained, wasn't private enough and he didn't have his own bathroom.

There would be several more moves before the Chases finally settled down permanently in the home they purchased after the success of *Harvey*.

Most people described Mary's marriage to Bob as successful. Given the fact that they would experience many separations and obstacles, their union could not help but experience some roadblocks. Still, they managed to remain together for fifty-three years until Mary's death.

In many ways, Robert Chase was a modern man. He was always supportive of his wife's interests and gladly helped to take care of his sons when it was necessary. But the marriage was still a traditional one. Mary was always referred to in news articles as Mrs. Robert Chase, and Bob, unless it was necessary, only assisted in taking care of the children. He didn't cook, and he didn't do laundry. In his spare time he was known to frequent the Denver Press Club and socialize with his cronies. He was highly regarded in the newspaper community. Even after Mary won the Pulitzer Prize for *Harvey*, she was still only recognized as a "housewife who wrote plays in her spare time."[7]

In an interview two years after *Harvey* debuted on Broadway, Mary commented on their marriage up to that point. "It's been a little tough on Bob. When I married him (one of the most capable and highly respected newspapermen in the Rocky Mountain Empire), I was scatter brained and willful; he had a reputation for integrity and endurance. He made it possible for me to write plays and I hope *Harvey* has made up somewhat for unmended socks and bad meals."[8]

7

THE HOUSEWIFE

Chase quit working for the *News* in 1931. She had worked for the *News* for seven years. Now it was time for a new chapter in her life.

LITTLE CHASES

From 1932 to 1936, Mary and Bob Chase welcomed three sons into the world: Michael Lamont in 1932, Colin Robert in 1935, and Barry Jerome in 1936.

In 1935, after the birth of their second child, the Chases moved from Mary's childhood home on West Fourth to a rental apartment on South Grant, where they lived for two years. After the birth of their third child, they moved again to a rented house on Fourteenth and Ash Street. In 1938 they moved once more to 1364 St. Paul where they resided for the next five years until they purchased their home on Circle Drive in 1945 after the success of *Harvey*.[1] The house on St. Paul was a warm, cozy, modest, two-story brick and stone bungalow similar to others on their tree-lined street. When the children reached school age, they attended the public school that was located near their home.

LIVING WITH THE TIMES

Though the country was in the midst of the dark days of the Great Depression, both Chases felt lucky to be able to afford to live in their new home. Despite their relative comfort, they still felt the impact of the times.

More than one-quarter of all wage-earning workers were unemployed. After President Herbert Hoover's philosophy of how to cure the woes of the country through a means of deregulation failed, Franklin Delano Roosevelt became the president in 1933 and offered some new alternatives. He created a multitude of government programs for suffering Americans to help the country get through the dark days. Chase's career as a playwright began as a result of a government program.

Roosevelt's optimism was reinforced by his wife, Eleanor, who proved to be an ardent spokesman for women and who inspired those of her gender of their importance and encouraged them to make contributions to society. In "My Day," her weekly *New York Times* column, Mrs. Roosevelt counseled women on domestic and civic issues and gave them a voice. The First Lady stressed that a woman needed employment "to do something that expresses her personality even though she may be a wife and mother."[2] Chase didn't seem to need any coaching. Nonetheless, she was still a fan.

At the *News* Bob was slowly advancing up the corporate ladder. As with most journalists, his salary was modest. The Chases were often in financial difficulty particularly because Mary Chase had a penchant for splurging impulsively especially on expensive hats and for doing so when funds were especially low. She was known to use her charm to stave off her creditors. Once she hired a photographer to take a photograph of her three children. It took her two years to pay off the photographer, but when she paid the final bill, the owner called to tell her how much she missed their conversations that they had had about their lives.

Nobody called Chase a good housekeeper. Dishes were always stacked in the sink, and layers of dust lined the shelves and the furniture. She frequently baked lemon meringue pies but those who tasted them were not inclined to ask her to repeat her effort.

The children had no difficulties with Mary's parenting. There were always stories at bedtime and freedom to get into all kinds of mischief. The boys all thought she was a good mom. Said Michael, her oldest son, "She was a marvelous parent."[3]

It was at bedtime that Mary's skills as a storyteller enjoyed their greatest moments. One can imagine wide eyes and giggles as Mary told them a story about a good boy named Ernest McGillacuddy and a bad boy named Roger O'Brien. Ernest always did what he was told and Roger, like her boys, always got in trouble for behaving badly. At the end there was always a moral and a positive message.

FREELANCING

To help supplement Bob's salary, Mary began to do some freelance work. From 1932 to 1936 she was contracted to write articles for the International News Service and the United Press.

Bob worked on the night shift and Mary, after she read her boys a few nighttime stories, returned to the dining room where she had set up a typewriter to write and where she began to think about pursuing some of her own ideas.

Her first attempt at becoming an author was a serious novel called *The Banshee* based on one of the myths told to her by her uncles when she was growing up. The banshee was a woman who carried with her a death omen. Whenever she was seen, she let out a horrible cry that legend said brought death to any family that heard it.

Mary's novel centered on Margaret who hears the wail of a banshee and mistakenly concludes that the death it forewarns will be that of her oldest son, the lover of a married woman. Margaret's meddling to prevent one son from being killed results in the ironic death of the other son.

After receiving several rejections for the submissions Mary sent to publishing houses, she shelved the novel. The year was 1934. More than ten years later after the premier of *Harvey*, she adapted the novel for what turned out to be a very brief theatrical run.

When her first attempt failed, she decided to see if she might have better luck writing a play. On the dining room table she set up a paper box stage and moved around empty thread spools to represent her characters. This first play, *Me Third*, was about politics and contained some of the humor that eventually became her voice in her future plays.

The inspiration for the play was a woman named Viola who was then working for the Chases as a part-time housekeeper and who had been an inmate at the state home for delinquent girls. It was further inspired, no doubt, by Mary's days as a newspaperwoman when she often covered crimes and corruption in government. Additionally the theme came from her family's and friends' interest in politics.

The story, *Me Third*, concerns a ne'er-do-well lawyer and his wife, a former bordello cashier, who hire a maid and a landscaper to make them look more impressive as a means of attracting the populace to vote for him for the office of district attorney. The wife falls in love with the landscaper and from that point on, the fun begins. It was intended to be a satire on politics, scandal, and prostitution with a moral of good conquers evil at the end. *Me Third* is the only Mary Chase play that includes a married woman, and it begins her recurring theme on the hypocrisy of the social climber. The title *Me Third* was taken from the ironic saying of her protagonist Harlan Hazlett: "God first, country second, me third."[4]

HAVING FUN

From the time that the Chases were first married, a mosaic of friends passed in and out of their homes. Many of their friends didn't know each other. Instead of the greenhorn friends that used to visit Mary's uncles, the guests that now came and went were newspaper and theater people like Kasper Monahan, drama critic of the *News*, Caroline Bancroft, the literary critic for the *Post*, and Selena Royle of the Elitch Theatre Stock Company. Discussions about fiery Denver Post owner F. G. Bonfils and Franklin Delano Roosevelt replaced arguments over Cromwell's politics.

For a while, Mary enjoyed a friendship with author Dorothy Parker, who had moved to Denver in 1934. The famous New York luminary, best known for her female presence at the Algonquin Roundtable of the 1920s and for witty sayings like "Men don't make passes at girls who wear glasses," had moved to Denver with her young boyfriend, Alan Campbell, who was enjoying a summer residency at the Elitch Theatre Stock Company.*

Parker loved being out of New York. In between writing some of her most noted work and doing some serious gardening, she confided to Mary and her friend and fellow journalist Caroline Bancroft that she thought Denver was a bit boring. She asked them to throw a party that included real people, not stuffed shirts. In response they rented a vacant house in Capitol Hill and invited twenty people to attend. The invitation list included a bootlegger, a prizefighter, and doyenne Louise Sneed Hill. Word got out to some of the locals who were not society folk and who ultimately crashed the party and allegedly made the party a lot more interesting. Even the governor attended.

Dorothy Parker called Mary the greatest undiscovered wit, a true compliment from a woman who was known herself to be a great wit.

A former *Rocky Mountain News* male editor of Mary's observed Mary's writing efforts this way:

> In due course Mary retired from newspapering. *Harvey* and her other plays were written amid the tumults of rearing three rowdy boys and the cross-bearing which goes with being the wife of a morning newspaperman, a pitiful situation of cold dinners, loneliness, social hibernation, and inattention, as the wife of any morning newspaperman will certify.[5]

That perception was to change.

---

*Elitch's was founded in 1891 and was the first summer stock company in the country. It spawned many well-known future celebrities including Edward G. Robinson, Harold Lloyd, and Fredric March.

ACT II

Mary Chase, Playwright

Settling down to a married life with children was a given assumption for Mary Chase. She had been raised in a loving and traditional family of modest means.

Though she had always been a rebellious youngster who craved attention, she still preferred to remain within the societal norms of the times, that of becoming a housewife and a mother who stayed at home to raise her children.

Still, she could not give up on the need to do more. She continued to write with the hidden hope of being recognized.

8

THE FEDERAL THEATRE PROJECT

America in the early 1930s was in deep pain. A lot of the money that had made life easier had disappeared and so had the gaiety. It was a time when the country's citizens were counting their blessings if they had a roof over their heads and ate three square meals a day.

In New York, the theater district was functioning but at a reduced level. Unlike Denver, New York audiences could still find a variety of choices. *The Ziegfield Follies* featured stars like Fanny Brice and Bob Hope. Musicals like *Girl Crazy* and *Porgy and Bess* and loony comedies like George S. Kaufman and Moss Hart's *You Can't Take It With You* attracted large audiences. Serious, sometimes controversial dramas by playwrights like Lillian Hellman (*The Children's Hour*) and Eugene O'Neill (*Long Day's Journey into Night*) were offered in the midst of the Great Depression.

For the rest of the country, radio occupied more of its time than theater. People regularly listened to programs that featured comedians Jack Benny and Fred Allen, Paul Whiteman's jazz band, and symphonies conducted by Arturo Toscanini. Shows like *Amos and Andy* (1928) and *The Goldbergs* (1929) kept them laughing. Frightening tales such as Orson Wells's *War of the Worlds* (1938) were popular choices as were westerns, mysteries, superhero tales, and soap operas. Those who could afford to pay admissions fees attended talking movies, which began in 1927.

The diminished theater scene put millions out of work and left a void for those who relied on the theater for their entertainment fulfillment.

The Franklin Delano Roosevelt administration wanted to create employment for the theatrical world and they wanted to offer a means of entertainment that would bring hope and comfort to a suffering population.

A NEW DEAL

In 1936 as part of the New Deal, the Works Progress Administration was formed to create jobs for nine million citizens who had lost their jobs during the Great Depression. People were hired to build highways, railroads, bridges, and electric lines that would simultaneously improve the country's infrastructure.

For those who were in the entertainment industry, funds were allocated to give work to every type of theater professional and offer a depressed country entertainment that would make them forget their troubles. The program was called the Federal Theatre Project (FTP).

The FTP advertised positions for every type of theater professional: seamstresses, stagehands, stage managers, electricians, musicians, directors, actors, set designers, set builders, makeup artists, and, yes, playwrights.

Cities in regions throughout the country were selected to be a part of the project, and Denver was one of those chosen. Theater productions at each regional theater were a combination of plays that had been performed in other cities as well as productions originating in each selected city. The FTP aimed at getting the entire country involved. For example, in New York there was a Yiddish Theatre on the Lower East Side for Jewish people and an African American Theatre in Harlem. Many artists got their starts with the FTP; among them were Orson Welles, Arthur Miller, the director Elia Kazan, and Mary Chase.

Some of the productions that came to Denver during the three-year run of the FTP included Shakespearean performances of *Macbeth*, *Julius Caesar*, and *Comedy of Errors* all at affordable prices. Also produced were W. S. Gilbert and Arthur Sullivan's *The Mikado*, Richard Brinsley Sheridan's *The Rivals* and *School for Scandal*, and children's theater productions of George Bernard Shaw's *Androcles and the Lion* and the tale of *Pinocchio*. Some vaudeville productions were also offered.

It was popular for a play to be produced at several different locations and then to rotate to another city. Sinclair Lewis's controversial play, *It Can't Happen Here*, a doomsday view of the future of America, was produced in eighteen cities simultaneously.*

The national director of the project was Hallie Flanagan, a professor of drama at Vassar College in Poughkeepsie, New York. Said Flanagan in her keynote statement about the program: "Our whole emphasis in the theatre enterprises which we are about to undertake should be on re-thinking rather than on remembering."[1]

Playwrights were encouraged to come up with hopeful themes and plots. There were strict guidelines on what the FTP was looking for. Flanagan

---

*Estimates of simultaneous productions throughout the country range from thirteen to twenty-two.

encouraged those who were applying to be a part of the project that they should not do "plays of a cheap, trivial, outworn or vulgar nature," but only "such plays as the government can stand proudly behind in a planned theatrical program, national in scope, regional in emphasis, and American in democratic attitude."[2]

Most of the playwrights whose work was chosen for production already had a track record or they came from the east. The possibility of a local playwright's play being produced was as remote as finding a six-foot-tall rabbit to be one's best friend.

Hallie Flanagan had the final say on what plays would be produced in all the cities. Chase never met her. She had to rely on local advocates to fight for her play to be accepted.

THE DENVER THEATER

Like the rest of the country, the Great Depression and the advent of the talkies drastically diminished the Denver legitimate theater scene. By 1929 most of the Curtis Street theaters had converted to movie palaces. The places where legitimate plays could be presented had been reduced to just a few in number and the audience was, for the most part, restricted to the wealthy. Popular Broadway fare made appearances in the summer at Central City outside of town and at the Elitch Stock Theatre Company. Touring companies brought the most current Broadway shows for limited engagements to the Orpheum, Broadway, and Auditorium theaters and continued to operate until the mid-1950s when they too closed their doors forever.

In answer to the departure of serious legitimate theater at the end of the 1920s, a new community theater was formed on the campus of the University of Denver. It was originally called the University Civic Theatre. The organizers were wealthy patrons in the community including Helen Bonfils, the daughter of *Denver Post* founder Frederick Bonfils, who in 1953 opened the first legitimate theater in forty years. Until the FTP was introduced, the University Civic Theatre was the only avenue available to aspiring playwrights who lived in Denver.

HOW ABOUT *ME THIRD?*

Chase passionately desired to have her play produced, and she seized on the opportunity that the FTP presented. In a later interview, she revealed how deeply she wanted to see her play come to life. "Oh, I had only one thing which I think is true of all playwrights. They want to see it [their play] on the stage in order to find out where they've been wrong and where they've hit and where they haven't."[3]

As a former newspaperwoman, Chase was up to date on all that was happening both nationally and locally in the theater world. She had reporter friends in the local arts community. From an early age she had followed the theater scene and regularly read the entertainment trade paper *Variety*.

When she heard about the Denver Theatre Project, she decided to submit *Me Third*, the play she had recently written, for consideration.

She began by visiting the Federal Theatre in downtown Denver. Located at 1447 Lawrence near the downtown theater district, the theater had gone through several evolutions. Originally it had been called the Baker Theatre and occupied an old telegraph building. It had started out as a burlesque theater complete with scintillating chorus girls. At one point it closed down and then became the home of several different religious sects. Now it was being spruced up as the Baker Federal Theatre.

The director chosen for the Denver Theatre Project was a local actor and director, Michael Andrew (Andy) Slane who had been an active participant at the University Civic Theatre.

One afternoon Chase, in her customary bold manner, decided it was time to meet Andy Slane. When they met, Andy thought he recognized something familiar about Chase. He asked her to come with him downstairs to the theater basement. He pointed to a large poster known as a "sheet" that highlighted a burlesque queen and behind her a chorus line of burlesque dancers. The headline read: "Miss Katie Coyle now appearing at the Pantages Theatre in San Francisco." It didn't take long for Chase to realize that the woman pictured on the sheet was her father's long-lost sister, Katie. There was a rumor in the Coyle family that Chase's father had a sister who nobody wanted to talk about. Later on Chase did connect with her aunt, but when she was introduced to the sheet, this was her first awareness of her Aunt Katie and her questionable presence. As Chase later explained, growing up it was "a disgrace" to be on stage.[4] It's possible that the reason she never told anyone about her desire to write for the theater was because Chase knew this assertion to be true.

Andy Slane became a tireless advocate for Chase. Being a local playwright in a town that was not known for its literary assets was a drawback to being accepted into the prestigious theatrical hierarchy. Chase either charmed Andy or convinced him that audiences would love *Me Third*.

To further increase her credibility, Chase hired Pat Duggan to be her agent. Duggan, Chase, and Andy Slane struck up an acquaintanceship with FTP regional director Howard Miller, who visited Denver frequently because his sister lived there. Howard Miller sent the script to Karon Tillman, Hallie Flanagan's assistant. He too liked the play and said the project committee would consider accepting it into production at their next meeting. It was decided that Andy Slane would go to the meeting and present the case for *Me Third* in person. The year was 1936.

Chase later said that Andy Slane was her ticket to Broadway. "My practical working theater education came from Andy Slane," she explained. "Andy knew everything."[5] Two years before her death in 1981, she told an interviewer, "It was Andy who taught me how to be a playwright."[6] She further explained that he was the one who helped her work with the actors so they would understand how to portray her scenes and characters. He insisted that she speak to him rather than directly to the actors. It was advice that she heeded for the remainder of time that she was writing plays.

PRESENTING *ME THIRD*

On November 28, 1936, *Me Third* was presented at the Baker Theater to an adoring audience:

> A capacity crowd, at least half of it swathed in furs and diamonds poured down to the WPA theatre at 1447 Lawrence Street. Just to make the event of the biggest opening in the history of any kind of a local theater, there were flowers galore for cast and author and music between acts by the Federal Music Project orchestra.[7]

Local newspapers rarely reviewed serious theater. Chase credits getting decent reviews for her play to the fact that she knew a lot of people in the newspaper business. Among them were the Chases' good friends, Peggy and Wallace Reef. Peggy was a WPA administrator, and Wally worked for the *Rocky Mountain News* and wrote for national publications.

It was the *Denver Post*'s opinion that *Me Third* was "hilariously funny, packing laugh upon laugh. . . . All in all, it looks as if we've got a hit on our hands—and in the home town too. [People] were surprised even those who knew she could write that she had a fine flair for plot and a feeling for fast paced dramatic style."[8]

"It was all perfect," Chase said in her 1979 interview about the FTP. "I felt like Cinderella going to the ball."[9] The shadows would come later.

Me Third went on to be produced by FTPs in San Francisco and Los Angeles to very receptive audiences. Ironically *Me Third* appeared in San Francisco at the Pantages Theatre, the same theater where Chase's Aunt Kate had originally starred in a burlesque show.

The FTP was only in existence for three years. Considerable objections were voiced by some of the members of Congress who thought some of the projects were too politically left-wing. The project closed its doors in 1939.

When asked many years later if she felt embarrassed by the fact that the FTP was a relief program and that it became somewhat tainted by many in the 1940s and 1950s when the House Un-American Activities Committee investigated many people in the entertainment industry, she replied in the negative. She thought the whole thing was just grand.

After *Me Third* was presented, Chase took a small acting role in *The Devil's Disciple* by George Bernard Shaw, another Baker Theatre production that occurred in the same season. It did not convince her to act rather than to be a playwright. Later she said that if she had acted, it might have made her a better playwright.[10]

Me Third bolstered Mary Chase's resolve. "It gave me my first feeling of success because it succeeded at the Baker Theatre and I did feel at home."[11]

Fueled by a positive reception, Chase decided to pursue the next step: getting her play to Broadway.

That would come to be, but not without unpleasant consequences.

9

THE BROADWAY FLOP

Feeling buoyant from her *Me Third* successes in Denver and on the road, Mary Chase spontaneously decided to pursue Broadway. "It just came to me, and I did it," she said later.[1]

Though she claimed to "know nothing about Broadway,"[2] she did know that Colorado native Antoinette Perry now lived in New York and was part of the Broadway theater scene. Occasional articles appeared in the local papers and in *Variety*, the entertainment trade paper, and focused on Perry's acting and directing successes. The *News* mentioned the fact that Antoinette Perry's mother lived in Denver. Chase adeptly assumed her former reporter skills, sought out Perry's mother's address, and then knocked on her door and asked for Perry's address in New York. Within a short period of time afterward, Chase sent Perry her *Me Third* manuscript. Always promoting, she also enclosed some clippings of the positive reviews from the play's recent March run at the Baker Theatre.

When Perry received Chase's manuscript, she passed it on to Brock Pemberton, a seasoned producer. She and Pemberton worked together frequently. She thought he might like the play, and Pemberton was known to have a soft spot for young playwrights.

THE "SKYLARK" TEAM
OF PERRY-PEMBERTON

Antoinette (Tony) Perry was born in 1888 in southern Colorado. She was the granddaughter of a state senator who threatened to cut off her inheritance when she said she wanted to become an actress. Nevertheless, she joined her aunt and uncle's traveling theater company at the age of sixteen. She was talented, beautiful, and possessed a soft and sweet disposition. Quickly she made her way to the New York stage first as a sought-after ingénue and then as a starring actress.

One night while she was appearing in a New York production touring Denver, Frank Frueauff, a Denver utility magnate, was in the audience and was beguiled by the enchanting Perry. He wooed her with candy and flowers and ultimately in 1909 they married. After the birth of their two daughters, he persuaded her to leave the stage entirely to raise their children in Denver. Frueauff's company later merged with the Cities Services conglomerate. The couple lived a glamorous life with homes in New York and Newport as well as in Denver. When Frueauff died suddenly in 1922, Perry packed up the family and moved back to New York to continue her acting career. Frueauff's estate had left her more than thirteen million dollars. She did not have trouble deciding that she would rather be on Broadway than playing bridge at a Denver mansion. She quickly resumed her prior status as an actress very much in demand.

While her husband was still living, Perry and Frueauff had developed a friendship with New York press agent turned producer Brock Pemberton. When she returned to New York, Perry became Pemberton's "angel" for many of his plays and, after she suffered a stroke and decided to turn her efforts to directing, the famous Perry-Pemberton partnership began. Their partnership turned out to be personal as well but as daughter Margaret Perry Fanning explained in a Playbill commemorating her mother, "Every night Pemberton went home to his wife and Tony went home to her two daughters."[3]

Years later Mary Chase became friends with Perry's daughter Margaret who followed in her mother's footsteps as an actress, played the maid in the New York production of *Me Third* (renamed *Now You've Done It* in New York), and eventually moved back to Denver to marry, raise a family, and continue her acting career.

Though Antoinette Perry distinguished herself in the theatrical world, and though she paved the way for women theater directors, she still remains best known for becoming the namesake of Broadway's prestigious Tony Awards that were created posthumously in her honor for her founding of the American Theatre Wing, an organization that supports the wellbeing of the theater and its actors. During World War II, the American Theatre Wing created a stage door canteen that provided entertainment for soldiers in a number of cities throughout the country and that later became the subject of a popular movie. The Tony Awards began in 1948 after her death at the age of fifty-eight in 1946. Said the actor Jesse White who played the character of Wilson, the burly sanitarium attendant in *Harvey* and later made his name selling Maytag washing machines: Antoinette Perry "was an angel of a woman."[4] *New York Times* drama critic Brooks Atkinson wrote: "Antoinette Perry was an imaginative, able and selfless person. There was nothing she would not or could not do. But fame was not what she was after. She just loved theater."[5]

Brock Pemberton, Perry's collaborator, had been producing on Broadway for almost twenty years when he accepted Chase's script. He was known for being a colorful character. Michael Chase, Chase's oldest son, later described him as a "bald-headed curmudgeon, tight fisted with money and gruff."[6] Pemberton was raised in Kansas and began his career as a journalist working for the iconic editor William Allen White at the *Emporia Gazette*. Despite his many years in New York, Pemberton maintained the practical values he had inherited from his Midwest upbringing and that he found to be present in Mary Coyle Chase's play.

Pemberton headed east to New York early in his career and became a press agent. He and his brother Murdock were frequent participants at the famous Algonquin Roundtable. After a while Pemberton decided to embark on a producing career. His first play, *Enter Madame*, was presented in 1920. Soon after in 1921 he produced the Pulitzer Prize–winning *Miss Lulu Bett* that was written by Zona Gale, the first woman to receive the award. Pemberton also gained recognition for bringing Luigi Pirandello's highly regarded play *Six Characters in Search of an Author* to America in 1924.

One of the first Perry-Pemberton collaborations, *Strictly Dishonorable* by playwright Preston Sturges, appeared in 1929 with Antoinette Perry directing and Brock Pemberton producing. The play was a major Broadway success with 557 performances and two succeeding film productions. Other play productions varied in degrees of success, but the team had built a reputation for light and entertaining fare known in the theater world as the Pemberton-Perry "skylarks."[7]

COME TO NEW YORK

When Brock Pemberton received Chase's *Me Third* script, he liked it immediately. Later Chase said that Brock "thought I had an instinct for the theater."[8] Pemberton's criteria for accepting plays for production was twofold: 1) Do I like the play? 2) Does it have a chance for success?

Pemberton called Chase and invited her to come to New York to rewrite the play and have it produced. Of course, she would have to take part of the financial risk for the play's production.

Producers of the time, like George Abbott and George S. Kaufman, charged playwrights 12 percent of the cost of the productions. Most of the productions during the 1930s and 1940s amounted to anywhere from twelve thousand to fifteen thousand dollars.[9] The Chases agreed that it was a gamble but they hoped to recover from their investment. Mary Chase was not going to miss her chance.

The offer took place during the Christmas season of 1936, just after her *Me Third* successful run at the Baker Theatre and five weeks after the Chases' third child, Barry Jerome, was born.

The first problem was childcare. Bob agreed to take on the task of caring for their infant son and their two- and five-year-olds. He had assistance from a woman Mary had hired to help with the household chores and the care of the children.

There was another obstacle. Somehow or another she had to pay for her train fare to get to New York, and she had to find a place to stay where she could rewrite the script and attend rehearsals. As was always true of the Chases, they were short of funds. Chase later said that she always thought, "Money was something you owed, not something you owned."[10] To pay for her expenses, the Chases took out a loan and sold their car.

In the midst of the Christmas season, Chase boarded the train to New York and settled in with a friend on New York's Upper East Side. Uncomfortable in her new surroundings and determined to work hard to make her play a success, she rarely left her room. In between rewrites and rehearsals, she spent most of her time corresponding with her husband about daily family issues and concerns.

The *New York Times* thoroughly enjoyed poking fun at Chase's hesitancy to mingle with New York luminaries:

> The Pemberton office thinks it is pretty remarkable. When its new author, Mary Coyle Davis (they didn't get it quite right) arrived from Denver 10 days ago to confer about her play, "Me Third" the Pemberton office was ready to grant her a little time. It was her first trip to New York, and, in cases like that the rules say that a visitor gets time to become acclimated—i.e. to see the sights. Not Mrs. Davis. She announced at once that she would lock herself in a hotel to write, and she did, and a little later she explained.
>
> It seems her husband, a Denver newspaperman, once accompanied the marble shooting champion of the University of Colorado to a national tournament in Atlantic City. It was the marble shooter's first trip East and he made the mistake of stopping off in New York and getting bewildered, so that he was no good at all when he got to Atlantic City and the Competition. Mrs. Davis has always allowed that nothing like that was going to happen to her.[11]

Working straight through the holidays, Chase made changes, and the production went into rehearsal. The title of the play became *Now You've Done It* after the other suggestions of *Pike's Peak* and *Pillows of Society* were dismissed. The original set was changed to a more glamorous brothel version based on a room at the Metropolitan Museum. The lawyer character, Harlan L. Hazlett, Jr., ran for Senate rather than district attorney.

Tony Perry directed and her daughter Margaret played the part of Grace Dosher, the maid on parole who is hired by the Hazletts to make them look more important.

Chase said that compared to her initial education from Andy Slane, at the Denver Federal Theatre Project, her time with Pemberton and Perry "was like graduate school." She said they were particularly interested in the set and also the scene structure. "They were interested in Broadway success, not in people outside of New York."[12]

There were a few problems. The opening had to be delayed when the title of the play was changed and four days before the opening, one of the actors had to have an emergency appendectomy and needed to be replaced. There may have been some other difficulties due to the fact that Tony Perry was working on two other plays at the same time.

Pemberton predicted a hit, and the signs were good. From rehearsals alone, offers for movie rights had been made, but Pemberton advised waiting until after the play opened.

Now You've Done It opened on March 5, 1937, at the Henry Miller Theatre in New York. It closed forty-three days later.

DISMAL REVIEWS

Said one critic from the *Brooklyn Eagle*, the play was "pedestrian with a will and elbow grease but no imagination."[13] Observed Books Atkinson of the *New York Times*: "*Now You've Done It*, Brock Pemberton's comedy serenade to spring, appears to be hackneyed in theme and laboriously written and staged and not one of the most light-winged of the Pemberton-Perry skylarks."[14]

Others declared the play "shrill and strained"[15] and "unimportant and preposterous."[16]

Despite the consensus of the critics, the audience seemed to love the play. Someone logged the number of laughs at 220.[17]

Robert Benchley of the *New Yorker* wrote that *Now You've Done It* "turned out to be pretty bad." He said it had "all the earmarks of a manuscript that one stops reading in the middle of the first act as an obvious waste of time," and that it was an "old story of sex hypocrisy among pious politicians never very funny even in the old days." He followed his diatribe with the statement: "I must admit, however, that the audience on the opening night seemed to adore it."[18]

Said producer Brock Pemberton, "A serpent's tooth is a blunt instrument compared to an unsuccessful play." And he further lamented in an interview, "Why must we let the critics in?"[19]

Mary Chase was stunned. She felt like the song "There's a Broken Heart for Every Light on Broadway" was written for her. Said Chase, "When you fail in the theater, it's a public disgrace."[20]

Chase decided that Broadway was not for her—that she "couldn't sit out in the Rockies and feel the pulse of Times Square."[21]

Many years later when Chase was asked why Denver did not produce more notable playwrights, Chase explained that it was just too hard to not be in New York where all the activity was centered. She also felt that there was a difference between a New York and a Denver audience. "So," she went on, "a sophisticated New York audience didn't respond in the same ways [as a] Denver audience did." She felt that the New York audience was "something different." She attributed some of that to the fact that in those days there was no television to make taste "more uniform."[22]

"You learn more from a flop than a success," she sighed. "Well, you have to get over it."[23]

A disheartened Mary Chase returned home to her Denver family and friends and resolved that she would never write for Broadway again.

Her failure on Broadway did quicken her fight. She was not going to let all those years of learning the technique of playwriting go unused. She would just write for her own satisfaction.

Pemberton could afford his losses more than could the Chases. Instead of returning from New York with a hoped-for nest egg, she came home badly in debt.

"We went for three years without an automobile to get out of debt. . . . The whole thing was a disaster . . . a terrific blow. I don't think I ever would have tried it again if Mr. Chase hadn't said to me, 'Write another play immediately. When a pilot crashes, they take him up in another plane before he leaves the field.'"[24]

Brock Pemberton also encouraged Mary to keep on writing.

10

TIME TO REGROUP

BACK TO DENVER

Humbled but not beaten, Mary returned to her Denver home and regrouped. She decided to concentrate on taking care of her young family, continuing to write, and contributing to her community.

From 1938 to 1941 Chase wrote three full-length plays and a one-act comedy.

SORORITY HOUSE

The first production after her 1937 flop was *Sorority House*. After her debut at the Federal Theatre Project, Chase had become a more attractive candidate to producers. When Chase suggested to the University Civic Theatre that they produce a play she had written called *Chi House*, they agreed to do so. The play was renamed *Sorority House* and was inspired by her unhappy experience when she tried to join a sorority at the University of Colorado. The play was produced in 1937.

In the play, a handsome big man on campus falls in love with a beautiful and brainy girl who has struggled to get to college and is not aware of sororities. Mr. Big attempts to woo the sorority girls to invite his girl to join by claiming she has hidden wealth. He even approaches the girl's father to see if he could provide the money needed to pay for her membership. Unknown to his daughter, the father sells his business. When he appears at the sorority house that has accepted her, she is embarrassed by his drab appearance and she sends him away. He retreats to her boardinghouse just in time to help out his daughter's roommate who has been

53

rejected and is having thoughts of suicide. After finding out that her father has sold his business so she can join a sorority, and with the approval of Mr. Big, the girl tears up the sorority's invitation and rejects all of the house's characteristics of pretension and snobbery.

Like her Federal Theatre Project production of *Me Third*, the reviews were glowing. The *Denver Post* said Chase had "another bulls-eye" and was "on her way to recognition as one of the foremost writers for the theater."[1] The recognition would remain in Denver.

As had been the case when *Me Third* was being produced, Chase was faced with tempting offers for *Sorority House*—one from a noted stage producer and another from RKO Films. Fearing that lightning might strike twice if she chose the stage route, Chase sold the rights of *Sorority House* to RKO for twenty-five hundred dollars. Dalton Trumbo, a fellow Coloradoan, co-wrote the screenplay. Trumbo was just beginning his screenwriting career writing screenplays for B movies, movies that were usually based on original plays or books and were quickly prepared for the screen. He later became famous for being sent to prison for refusing to give information to the House Un-American Activities Committee, for being blacklisted by the movie industry, and, after that, for achieving acclaim for such blockbuster movies as *Exodus* and *Spartacus*. Trumbo had grown up in Grand Junction, Colorado, and had attended the University of Colorado at around the same time Chase did.

The movie *Sorority House* debuted in 1939 and starred Anne Shirley who had achieved fame in *Anne of Green Gables*. The reviews were tepid.

Said the *New York Times* in its review:

> Thankful as we ever are for small favors, we must acknowledge our indebtedness to the Palace's *Sorority House* for a new word, "dreep." It would be listed in the dictionary thus: "Dreep, n. colloq.; a combination of dreary and weep; used to designate female students at Talbot University who have not been elected to membership in any of the sororities." Hoisting RKO by its own petard, *Sorority House* is a "dreep."[2]

The amount and the success of the film was modest. But at least the Chases were able to replace their car and buy new draperies.

MORE PLAYS AND SCRIPTS

After she had completed her work on *Sorority House*, Chase turned her energies to a variety of projects.

In 1938, she wrote a series of scripts for a weekly radio program entitled *Colorado's Hour*, a combination of historic travelogues and descriptions of current events for various Colorado towns and counties.

Chase completed writing another play in 1939 that was never produced. It was called *Colorado Dateline*. The plot centered on a rookie reporter who loses her objectivity and becomes involved with the accused in a murder trial.

Too Much Business, a one-act comedy, came next. It was set in a movie house full of raucous kids similar to the ones she was taking care of at her own home. The play was also staged at the University Civic Theater in 1941.

After the United States entered World War II in 1941, Chase wrote *A Slip of a Girl*, a musical comedy, to entertain the Tenth Mountain Division of troops training for battle at nearby Camp Hale.

MARY, THE HUMANITARIAN

During her "recovery" period, Chase also turned her attention to her community. In between her writing efforts, she became a dedicated defender of human rights.

She served as the Information Director for the National Youth Administration, a New Deal agency sponsored by President Franklin Delano Roosevelt that focused on providing work and education for Americans between the ages of sixteen and twenty-five. She wrote weekly radio programs for the Teamsters' Union and supported Spanish-American sugar beet workers and oleomargarine laborers in their efforts to achieve equal pay and equal rights.

For each effort, Chase showed up at demonstrations wearing a big hat, a slinky black dress, and dangling earrings. In her usual vamping fashion, she hoisted a picket sign and marched with supporters. Sometimes she served sandwiches to others marching and used her charm on the police to let laborers' protests continue.

Her husband, Bob, during this time was active in organizing the Denver chapter of the American Newspaper Guild to protect news reporters and editors. Mary assisted him in supporting the cause.

Whatever the Chase family lacked in financial comfort was compensated for by a rich family life, a legion of friends, and a passion to serve their community.

Chase had recovered from the pain of her abysmal experience with *Me Third*. Knowing that she was happiest when she was writing, she continued to churn out manuscripts and then try to find a place where her plays could best be presented.

11

THE POOKA

WHAT TO DO IN WARTIME

When Japanese air forces attacked Pearl Harbor on December 7, 1941, Americans joined the Allies and entered World War II. Before the war was over in 1944, sixteen million Americans donned uniforms, and millions more Americans stayed home and assisted in various roles needed to support the war effort.

Whether you were on the front lines or at home, it was difficult not to feel the impact of the war.

Mary and Bob Chase's children were now of school age. Michael was nine, Colin was six, and Jerry was five. Bob at this point was serving at the *News* as city editor working at night from 5:00 p.m. to 1:00 a.m.

Each day Chase prepared to walk her boys the seven blocks to their school and each day before they began, she would see a woman who lived in an apartment building across the street come out the door and walk sadly to the streetcar stop nearby. Word was out that the woman was a widow and that she had recently received a black-bordered telegram announcing that her only son had been killed in combat. Though Chase did not know the woman personally, she could not help but feel the woman's grief. Here she was safely walking her boys to school and the woman had lost her only son.

Each day the widow's gait lessened as she started her workday and each day Chase thought more about what she could do to make this woman and the country in general laugh again.

For three months Chase kept trying out ideas and rejecting them. Should she write a play about sex? No. Money? No. Politics? No. What could possibly make this woman laugh? Chase grasped for ideas. As she was prone to do when clearing her mind, she went into her closet and prayed.

THE DREAM

Then about five o'clock one morning she awoke from a dream about a psychiatrist being chased by a giant white rabbit and she knew she had it. This would be the story and now all she had to do was fill in the details. It was time to go to work.

THE LEGEND OF THE POOKA

As a child Chase had heard many stories about a large mythical animal called a pooka that appeared as a horse, a goat, a dog, and a rabbit. Regardless of what form they took, pookas were known for spreading all kinds of mischief but in the long run for being benevolent souls.

On a good day the pooka caused destruction on a farm—tearing down fences and disrupting the animals. On a bad day, the pooka stood outside the farmhouse and called the people outside by name. If anyone came out, the pooka carried them away. The pookas also loved to confuse the ships pulling away from Ireland, and they were blamed for many shipwrecks along the rocky coast.[1]

"Hmm," thought Mary. "What kind of havoc can I create for my pooka?"

TWO YEARS AT THE TYPEWRITER

It took Chase two years to complete the manuscript she called "The Pooka."

At various stages of her writing, the characters took different shapes. Instead of a rabbit, she tried a man-sized canary. At one point the lead protagonist became a female and she envisioned the illustrious actress Tallulah Bankhead in the lead role. Finally she settled on a six-foot, one-and-a-half-inch male rabbit and his friend, Elwood P. Dowd.

Theories exist that she patterned Elwood after two gentlemen she knew. One was her brother Charlie who had had difficulty meeting reality, and the other was Lee Casey, a fellow *News* reporter and columnist with a gentle soul.*

Every night after her children went to sleep and her husband went to work, Chase pounded away in her dining room on her typewriter. While she listened to the radio blaring news of the details of World War II battles and subsequent casualty counts, she moved her thread spool characters back and forth inside the paper box stage set of the imaginary Dowd library and the Chumley Rest Sanitarium.

---

*Various versions attest to others who might have inspired Elwood including Chase's father and the *Rocky Mountain News* photographer Harry Rhoads.

Chase was now deft at her craft. She had settled on the idea of writing comedies and knew what kinds of techniques to use to make people laugh. The story had to have a "heart-line," some universal thought to convey to the audience, and it must contain elements of love, laughter, and beauty.

In much the same way as the pooka went through many identities, so did the characters and the circumstances of the play. This was helped along by her readings of the play to those around her, including the cleaning woman.

Essentially the plot remained the same. Elwood P. Dowd's friend Harvey, an imaginary rabbit, proves to be an embarrassment for Elwood's sister, Veta, and her daughter, Myrtle Mae, who are trying very hard to find a respectable mate for Myrtle Mae. When Elwood embarrasses the two at a society tea by introducing Harvey to a relative who is a society matron and distant relative, Veta vows to have Elwood committed to a sanitarium. Once she goes to have him committed there is confusion as to who is the patient and Veta winds up being committed instead. In the second scene at Chumley's Rest Sanitarium we are introduced to Dr. Sanderson, the assistant psychiatrist, his nurse, Miss Kelly, and Wilson, the attendant at the sanitarium. Veta, who is now restrained, calls up her friend Judge Gaffney to get her out of this situation, and she is finally released after experiencing a great deal of abuse. The lead psychiatrist, Dr. Chumley, takes over the case to try and straighten things out and becomes enamored with Elwood and his friend Harvey. Still the plans are made to give Elwood a Formula 977 shot that will make Elwood normal again. Only at the last minute does Veta decide that rather than make him like everyone else, she loves her brother the way he is.

While Chase was writing *Harvey*, the children were either left to amuse themselves or supervised by a part-time housekeeper. They did not complain. It was an opportunity to get away with all kinds of mischief. When their mom was writing she was rarely "present."

"Ask her now," coaxed Jerry. "She'll say yes."[2]

Knowing that their mother was writing a play about Harvey, the invisible rabbit, a request to put away their toys or hang up their coats was often greeted with the response: "Harvey will do it." The boys were busy burying her silver in the backyard.

Regardless of Chase's preoccupation, her children didn't seem to feel neglected. It is true that buttons were sometimes missing from their shirts and oftentimes they needed haircuts. For the most part, life remained normal.

Chase too was a little disheveled during this time. She often needed a permanent wave. She smoked constantly, and she lived on large pots of coffee.

Her husband didn't complain. He worked just as hard as his wife did. The house had a rhythm to it.

After two years Chase completed "The Pooka." It was time to call Brock Pemberton again. She had forgotten about her vow never to return to Broadway. She decided her story needed to be told. She was determined to make that widow laugh again.

12

BACK TO BROADWAY

Within two years after Mary was awakened by a nightmare about a tall white rabbit chasing a psychiatrist, she had completed the play that grew out of that strange dream. The name of the play was changed from "The Pooka" to *The White Rabbit.*

In the spring of 1944, she sent the script off to producer Brock Pemberton in New York. She felt it was worth taking the chance to return to Broadway if she could create a comedy that would bring laughter to the woman who lived across the street and to a country suffering from war fatigue. She had no regrets about her turnabout decision. Where else could she make as many people as possible try to laugh during this very sad time?

Along with the manuscript, Chase included some directions on her perception of how the play should be presented. "It must be bold humor with a folklore quality to it," she told Pemberton. "The laughs must be rooted in truth."[1]

Pemberton was thrilled to receive the manuscript. He had once complained that playwrights usually were not particularly loyal and preferred to seek the best offer, especially if their first attempt had not been a success. It had also been a few years since the Pemberton-Perry team had had a big hit. With the exception of *Kiss the Boys Good Bye*, a spoof on *Gone With the Wind*, and *Janie*, which was bought up by the movies, it had been a rather dry spell since their more successful plays that had produced large numbers of performances and good reviews.

After she sent the manuscript to Pemberton, Chase resumed her normal routine of caring for her three boys, now twelve, nine, and eight, leading a normal married life, and figuring out what her next writing project would be.

One night, soon after Chase sent Pemberton the manuscript, she was reading her children a bedtime story when she received a phone call from Pemberton.

Chase interrupted the reading to take the call. Pemberton told her he liked the script of *The White Rabbit* and wanted to produce it. They chatted for quite a while on the phone, and when Chase returned to her boys to finish the story, they were all fast asleep. Chase was sure the book she had been reading her children was a good luck charm.

FINDING BELIEVERS

When Brock Pemberton showed *The White Rabbit* script around, most dismissed the story itself and Pemberton's plan to produce it as preposterous. Who would believe that an amiable lush like Elwood P. Dowd could have an invisible six-foot, one-and-a-half-inch-tall white rabbit for a friend? And, in fact, why would anybody care?

Not even Pemberton's wife or Antoinette Perry was in favor of Pemberton's choice. When Pemberton approached some potential backers he got a variety of responses, but very few were positive. The head of one booking agency actually took the script to his psychiatrist, who said the play glorified a drunk. Preston Sturges, the highly successful playwright and well-respected film director, declared Pemberton himself to be crazy if he produced the play. Only a ticket seller with limited funds was positive. But Pemberton persisted and was eventually able to convince the most important people—his wife and his partner—that the play should be made. From there he found the money and turned his efforts toward casting.

CASTING *HARVEY*

After Pemberton procured financial backing, the production process was set into motion. Perry began to work on the staging, and she and Pemberton found a designer and hired the production staff. Throughout this period, Chase continued to make some preliminary changes to the script.

In the meantime, work began on casting the production. Who should play the kind, adaptable, and charming Elwood? Who would be able to convince the audience that his best friend was an invisible six-foot, one-and-a-half-inch rabbit?

Pemberton had fifty actors on his list of possibles. He wanted the biggest names out there that would draw the most attention and heighten interest in the play. At the top of the list he placed the names of silent screen star Harold Lloyd and actor Jack Haley who was in the public's mind after his recent performance as the Tin Man in the 1939 hit film *The Wizard of Oz*. Both of them said no. Lloyd didn't think the play was funny enough.

During the time he was casting *The White Rabbit*, Pemberton made a trip to San Francisco in search of a site for the touring company of *Janie*, his current play on Broadway. He met an old friend, a banker, for dinner and told him about his frustration in trying to find someone to play Elwood. His friend recommended Frank Fay, who had introduced comedy to vaudeville and had starred in a number of successful comedy films in the 1930s. Fay's career had taken a downhill turn after his former wife, Barbara Stanwyck, became a star, and he had overspent on properties and over-imbibed alcohol. (It is said that the Fay-Stanwyck relationship was the inspiration for the first filming of *A Star is Born* in 1937. The film was remade for the third time in 2018.) Fay was now a reformed alcoholic and was living in a deteriorating mansion in Los Angeles, trying to keep up with the bills in between doing occasional nightclub stints around the country.

"Hmmm," ruminated a skeptical Pemberton. But he did go to see Fay when he came to New York to perform at the Copacabana, and invited him to dinner and to do an informal reading for Elwood. Fay's own Irish heritage, his life as a comedian, and his close acquaintance with alcohol served as a natural background for his casual audition. The day after the dinner, Fay called Pemberton. "Brock," he said, "I'm your boy if you'll have me."[2] It was settled. Frank Fay was chosen to play the role of Elwood P. Dowd.

There was no such difficulty casting Veta, Elwood's social-climbing sister. No one doing Broadway at that time was more popular than Josephine Hull. Short, stout, jittery, and adorable, Ms. Hull had recently been lauded for her performance in the 1941 stage production of *Arsenic and Old Lace*, and she was currently starring with Cary Grant in the 1944 film production of the play. Hull was already in her sixties when she took on the role of Veta. Chase solved that problem by raising the age given in the script description of her character from forty to forty-eight.

Pemberton took a chance on casting the strongman Wilson in the play with Jesse White, a newcomer to the stage. Veteran performers easily filled the roles of the other characters.

THE REWRITES

Brock Pemberton was amazed at the deep-rooted structure of Chase's play. He said she knew playwriting inside out and upside down.[3] Despite that fact, the play still went through sixteen major rewrites and a name change before the final script was settled in place.[4]

While waiting to travel to New York for the final weeks of rewriting and rehearsals followed by the Boston tryout, Chase made childcare arrangements for her boys once again. Plans were made for oldest son, Michael, and the family springer spaniel, Joe, to stay with a friend and for the younger two boys to move in with Mary's sister, Katherine. Bob could fare for himself at the house on St. Paul Street.

Six weeks before the New York curtain was scheduled to rise on *The White Rabbit*, Chase boarded the train for New York. This time she and Bob did not have to sell their car to get her there. Her train ticket came out of the five hundred dollar advance Pemberton had sent to her, and Pemberton and Perry settled her into the Algonquin Hotel for the final weeks of preparation.

Every morning Chase arrived at Antoinette Perry's spacious Park Avenue apartment and took a seat at a table in Perry's forty-five-foot-long living room that also housed three pianos. For the remainder of the day until seven or so at night, the cast and crew would address each act and scene and make adjustments as needed.

Should Elwood carry a coat for Harvey in scene 2 when he enters Chumley's Rest Sanitarium? How about if he carries his hat as well? That hat would have to have holes for Harvey's ears. Are those realtors in the first act who appear at the Dowd house necessary? It might be better to eliminate them and just discuss that they are looking at the house and hear them rumbling around upstairs.

The Perry-Pemberton team was known for their rewrites, but their actors were not allowed to make changes, though Frank Fay tried. Perry was known for making the scenes move quickly. Pemberton concentrated on dialogue and relied on Perry's acting expertise for guidance.

It was Pemberton who added Dr. Chumley's line when, after Elwood learns that his sister wants him committed to Chumley's Rest, he confoundedly asks him, "Don't you have the courage of your convictions?" Elwood responds: "Years ago my mother used to say to me, she'd say, 'In this world, Elwood—she always called me Elwood—you must be . . . oh so smart or oh so pleasant.' For years I was smart. I recommend pleasant. You may quote me."[5]

On a daily basis, the dynamics among cast and crew were less than calm. Frank Fay, often childish in his antics, always needed a lot of attention. He either created it or demanded it. Remembering what her first teacher, Andy Slane, had taught her during her debut Federal Theatre production of *Me Third*, Chase let the process unfold, and only when she had serious reservations did she channel those through Antoinette Perry. But she did plenty of venting to her friends and family at home.

A week before the Boston tryouts, one of Frank Fay's suggestions was finally accepted. Instead of *The White Rabbit*, he thought the name of the play should be *Harvey*. Everyone agreed.

LONELY FOR HOME

Suffering from migraine headaches and constant worries about the rewrites as well as the ups and downs going on in her family, Chase swayed between the excitement of having her play produced and the frustration of plodding through the tasks at hand. Occasional calls from the family gave her comfort, as did letters like ones from Bob, her son Colin, and friends, all expressing support and sympathy.[6]

September 30, 1944, Algonquin Hotel
"You didn't expect those people in New York to have any fresh viewpoints did you? Any ideas which are new or different come from the grass roots country, not from the big trending cities. New York should be a place to exchange ideas."
—Bob Chase

October 3, 1944, Algonquin Hotel
"Dear Mary,
Your boys are fine and seem very happy so please don't worry about them. Mike has a teacher he doesn't like. He has a good appetite. He joined the swimming team. He liked it the first day but didn't like it the second week."—Lucille Vidal, friend

October 4, 1944, Algonquin Hotel
"Should the boys be taking cod liver oil? I love you and miss you very much. . . . That rabbit suit sounds swell."—Bob Chase

October 5, 1944, Algonquin Hotel
"Don't let them get you down."—Mrs. Charles Peavy, friend

October 6, 1944, Algonquin Hotel
"Mike finally got to swim today. I think I was more thrilled than Mike. . . . I'm taking typing. I've stayed home long enough."—Lucille Vidal, friend

October 8, 1944, Algonquin Hotel
"Mary, do you think Brock could advance us a little bit more money?"
—Bob Chase

October 8, 1944, Algonquin Hotel
[On lined paper with a heart and an arrow]
"Dear Mom,
I love you and miss you very much."—Colin (age nine), son

October 9, 1944, Algonquin Hotel
"I think we agree New York is not the place to raise these boys—and I really am not looking for a nice throat-cutting setup in any event. It's easy enough to get your throat slashed these days without looking around for it."—Bob Chase

October 10, 1944, Copley Hotel, Boston
"Dear Mary,
Try to stay calm. I think those grandstanding so and so's are worth the bother. . . . I love you and miss you."—Bob Chase

THE BOSTON TRYOUT

The Boston tryouts began at the Copley Theatre on October 10 and lasted ten days. For opening night Mary donned a borrowed dress and stuffed the bottom of her shoes with paper to keep from feeling the holes in them. It is difficult to know whether she had neglected to buy something new or whether she was trying to save money.

Some positive signs had begun to make her feel hopeful about the play's outcome. Josephine Hull had given her a four-leaf clover, and another member of the cast had given her a two-dollar bill. As a truck driver pulled his rig up next to the cab that was dropping her off at the theater, he turned his head toward her and casually said, "Hello, luv." Chase took this as a benediction. She was going to have a hit.[7]

Bob had sent one more letter from home before the opening: "Don't be unhappy if the play does not succeed," he told her. "You still have your husband and your three boys, and they all love you."[8]

Perry, Pemberton, and Chase entered the Copley Theatre and took their seats. The curtain rose on the set of the library of the old Dowd family mansion, with the warbling sounds in the background of a woman's voice singing, "I'm Called Little Buttercup," a signal to the audience that for the next two hours, life was going to have some entertaining moments.

All the positive signs Mary had clung to before entering the theater that evening for the first performance were correct: the laughs were consistent, the applause thunderous, and the curtain calls numerous.

THE FIRST REVIEWS

Reviews from the Boston papers the next morning were all positive:

> "Harvey is a play with a spiritual message in farce terms."—Leo Gaffney, *Boston Record*

> "One of the earth's most beautiful people."—*Boston Globe* (referring to Elwood)

> "[Mary Chase's] deft parrying of realism with logic carried to its ultimate fantasy."—*Boston Globe*

> "[Chase's fantasy is] stated in so sweetly reasonable a fashion that you emerge from the theater . . . nearly convinced that it all happened."—*Boston Herald*[9]

The day after the opening of the Boston preview, Frank Fay called Chase on the phone. "Mrs. Chase," he said, "I think you've got a hit on your hands." "Are you sure?" she asked uncertainly. Frank Fay, known to be outspoken and outrageous, responded, "You are a dumb Denver housewife!"[10] Frank's tease relaxed the tension they had both felt during the entire time they'd worked together on the play's preparations. Despite his idiosyncrasies, his comment paved the way for their long and lasting friendship.

SHOULD HARVEY BE REAL?

Chase had told Brock Pemberton that if Harvey did not make one real appearance on stage, she was going to take the manuscript away from him. Chase felt strongly that a real appearance of Harvey would dispel the notion that the only reason Elwood sees Harvey is because he's inebriated.

Almost everyone was against Harvey's appearance, but to appease Chase, Pemberton hired a marionette maker to design a rabbit costume. It did not arrive until the end of the Boston tryout. To test out Harvey's real appearance on stage, a special performance was given to an audience of military men. A stage manager suited up with the finished costume and the experiment began.

Harvey made his first "real" appearance at the end of the second act when Dr. Chumley returns from his meeting with Elwood and Harvey at Charlie's Bar.

The audience was dumbfounded when they met the real rabbit. Here was a tall figure dressed in a rabbit skin that reminded people more of the Big Bad Wolf than a fuzzy, friendly Peter Cottontail. He didn't fit with how they pictured him. It was almost like there was a gasp from the audience when this odd version of Harvey made his entrance. Once the real Harvey left the stage, there was a sigh of relief and the laughs began again. It seemed like the audience preferred to use their own imaginations rather than see the real rabbit. Harvey made one more appearance at the end of the play when he and Elwood were reunited as they left the set and headed once again to Charlie's Bar.

After this uncomfortable presentation, Pemberton and Frank Fay finally were able to convince Chase that the appearance of a real Harvey in the play was not going to work. She mostly gave in, but Harvey still took one more live curtain call before he was permanently banned from appearing. The $650 costume was retired for good, and the image of Harvey was destined to live only in audiences' imaginations.

Once that decision was made, additional actions and dialogue were added to reinforce the invisible existence of Harvey. At the end of the second act, for example, doors opened by themselves, and then, after a ten-second pause, they mysteriously closed themselves. On the last day of the Boston tryout, Chase also added a line at the end of act 1, scene 2, to further assure that Harvey's presence was evident when she has Mr. Wilson, the sanitarium attendant, look up and read the definition of a pooka in the encyclopedia: "P-o-o-k-a. Pooka. From old Celtic mythology. A fairy spirit in animal form. Always very large. The pooka appears here and there, now and then, to this one and that one at his own caprice. A wise but mischievous creature. Very fond of rum-pots, crack-pots, and how are you, Mr. Wilson?"[11] Mr. Wilson looks at the book in surprise and asks who in the encyclopedia wants to know how he's feeling.

The time had come to move on to Broadway. The luck of the Irish was in the air.

13

IT'S A HIT!

Harvey opened at the 48th Street Theatre on November 1, 1944, at 8:00 p.m. Whether or not it was coincidence, the first of November in Irish lore is the beginning of the month of the pooka. In attendance were a very nervous Mary Chase and her husband, Bob, who had just arrived in New York from Denver.

PRESENTING *HARVEY*

The curtain rose on the set of the aging grandeur of the Dowd library. Myrtle Mae entered to take a phone call from the local society editor, and then called in her mother to speak to the editor:

> VETA. This is Veta Simmons. Yes—a tea and reception for the members of the Wednesday Forum.[1]

After a brief conversation with the society editor, Veta hangs up the phone, and she and Myrtle Mae discuss their unhappiness about Elwood and his invisible rabbit friend Harvey and then leave the room. Soon, Elwood enters and we meet him for the first time. He is described as:

> *(a man about 47 years old with a dignified bearing, and yet a dreamy expression in his eyes. His expression is benign, yet serious to the point of gravity. He wears an overcoat and a battered old top hat. This hat, reminiscent of the Joe College era, sits on top of his head. Over his arm he carries another hat and coat. As he enters, although he is alone, he seems to be ushering and bowing someone else in with him. He bows the invisible person over to a chair. His step is light, his movements quiet and his voice low-pitched.)[2]*

ELWOOD. *(To invisible person.)* Excuse me a moment. I have to answer the phone. [before it rings] Make yourself comfortable, Harvey. *(Phone rings)* Hello. Oh you've got the wrong number. But how are you anyway? This is Elwood P. Dowd speaking. I'll do? Well thank you. And what is your name, my dear? I would be happy to join your club.[3]

It only takes the opening moments for the audience to become enchanted with Elwood. He's just so nice.

For two hours the audience is treated to a play that is rooted in the truth and contains all the elements of laughter, love, and beauty.

The laughter abounds as Elwood maneuvers Harvey around the stage much to the dismay of all who meet him. There is humor in Veta's mistreatment at the sanitarium and in her outrage, "All you guys think about is sex."[4] Beauty surfaces in Elwood's kindness and in Dr. Chumley's eventual ability to "smell the roses." Love takes place in the form of Elwood's encouragement of Nurse Kelly and Dr. Sanderson to become closer, and in a blooming relationship between Wilson and Myrtle Mae and when Veta realizes how much she loves her brother and doesn't want him to change.

The truth is rooted in the dialogue made by the various characters.

Nurse Kelly asks Elwood what he does that makes him need to be going (to Charlie's bar) and Elwood responds:

Harvey and I sit in the bars and we have a drink or two and play the jukebox. Soon the faces of the other people turn toward mine and smile. They are saying: "We don't know your name, Mister, but you're a lovely fellow." Harvey and I warm ourselves in all these golden moments. We have entered as strangers—soon we have friends. They come over. They sit with us. They drink with us. They talk to us. They tell about the big terrible things they have done. The big wonderful things they *will* do. Their hopes, their regrets, their loves, their hates. All very large because nobody ever brings anything small into a bar. Then I introduce them to Harvey. And he is bigger and grander than anything they offer me. When they leave, they leave impressed. The people seldom come back—but that's envy my dear. There's a little bit of envy in the best of us—too bad, isn't it?[5]

Veta comments on the subject of reality and illusion:

I took a course in art this last winter. The difference between a fine oil painting and a mechanical thing like a photograph is simply this: a photograph shows only the reality: a painting shows not only the reality but the dream behind it—It's our dreams that keep us going. That separate us from the beasts. I wouldn't even want to live if I thought it was just eating and sleeping and taking off my clothes. Well—putting them on again.[6]

The cab driver E. J. Lofgren laments in the final scene about the changes that take place after patients have been inoculated with the Formula 977 to make them normal:

I've been drivin' this route fifteen years. I've brought 'em out here to get that stuff and drove 'em back after they had it. It changes 'em. . . . On the way out here they sit back and enjoy the ride. They talk to me. Sometimes we stop and watch the birds when there ain't no birds and look at the sunsets when it's rainin'. We have a swell time and I always get a big tip. But afterward . . . they crab, crab, crab. They yell at me to watch the lights, watch the brakes, watch the intersection. They scream at me to hurry. They got no faith—in me or my buggy—yet it's the same cab—the same driver—and we're goin' back over the very same road. It's no fun—and no tips.[7]

Finally the curtain fell as Elwood and Harvey reunited. When the cast took its bows, they were greeted by the roaring and continuous applause of an adoring and enchanted audience.

In the lobby afterwards, Mary could hear the comment that made her the happiest: "The first time Mother laughed since Joe was killed," offered a pleased member of the audience.[8]

RAVE REVIEWS

The reviews were even more euphoric than they were in Boston.

John Chapman of the *Daily News* thought it "the most delightful, droll, endearing, funny and touching piece of stage whimsy I ever saw."[9]

Time crowned it the funniest fantasy Broadway "has seen for years."[10]

Burton Rascoe in the *World-Telegram* couldn't recall another opening where he laughed "so hard and so continuously. . . . The whole fantasy is delicious, subtle, clever and very funny."[11]

Six weeks after *Harvey*'s debut, a columnist indicated what a sell-out hit *Harvey* had become: "I met Harvey the other night. Frank Fay introduced us in a play called *Harvey*, dreamed up by Mary Chase and enshrined at the 48th Street Theatre. Try to get in between now and the Fourth of July. I was quite comfortable on the left prong of a chandelier."[12]

HARVEY ACOLYTES

Everyone wanted to see *Harvey*. It became the thing to do.

For a long time after its opening, the phantom Harvey was openly received wherever he went. Frank Fay's dressing room was full of photos of rabbits. Admirers often sent him live ones as well. A setting with carrots and a martini regularly awaited Harvey at Frank Fay's table at the famous New York restaurant Toots Shor's. Chase received photographs of people wearing Harvey costumes at masquerade parties.

THE SUCCESS OF *HARVEY*

Harvey played for four and a half years and clocked in 1,775 performances. It was one of the longest running plays ever to appear on Broadway. In 1948, it traveled to London for two years where it played at the Theatre Royal Birmingham and at the Prince of Wales Theatre. It toured Denmark, Sweden, Australia, Japan, and throughout Europe, and it was translated into many languages. "The only ones who didn't understand *Harvey* were the French,"[13] observed Chase. They could not imagine a man winding up in a relationship with a rabbit rather than a woman.

Of the two theater awards given at the time, *Harvey* won the Pulitzer Prize for Best Drama. The Drama Critics' Circle Award went to Tennessee Williams for his play *The Glass Menagerie.*

Frank Fay was awarded the Drama Critics' Circle Award for Best Actor in a Broadway play. Josephine Hull received a Drama Critics' Circle Award for Best Actress in a Supporting Role.

In the four and a half years of its run, seven actors played the role of Harvey, but Frank Fay played in more performances than any of the others. Second after him was a young actor named James Stewart who went on to play Elwood in the movie. The comedian Joe E. Brown starred in the touring company.

Josephine Hull gladly played Veta for the first three years of the Broadway production. For the final year and a half, comedian Marian Lorne took over the role of Veta before the play finally came to Denver in 1947.

Jesse White continued to act in the role of Wilson for all four and a half years and went on to re-create his character in the movie.

Altogether there were three touring companies, two in the United States and one in London, England.

THE YEAS AND THE NAYS

Who deserves the credit for the success of *Harvey* continues to be a subject of discussion. One contingent believes the play's success was due to the fact that it allowed the actors to showcase their talents. Another group supports the notion that the play was helped along by the times and that people were looking for escape. Still others disapprove of Harvey's aberrant behavior and his opposition to society's norms.

Only a few give credit to the playwright for creating a well-crafted play in which the laughter implies an underlying universal meaning of kindness, humanity, tolerance, and love that continues to endure.

Abe Laufe in his book *Anatomy of a Hit* asserted that *Harvey*'s success had little to do with anything more than the fact that it was good escapism.

"Audiences did not come to see *Harvey* for the educational value they might find in the characterization of an amiable alcoholic who is more desirable than his sober companion. They supported the play because it provided entertainment and good entertainment at that, in a well-acted farce that avoided war themes and gave an opportunity to laugh at sobriety."[14] He added, "The tremendous popular appeal of the play was also due in part to the booming World War II years when *Harvey* played on Broadway. The comedy amused audiences who crowded the New York theaters in search of humor and escapism."

Laufe attributed the success of *Harvey* more to the portrayal of the characters of Veta and Elwood than to the structure and craft of the play itself. "Audiences for the most part did not take Elwood or the play seriously. They enjoyed watching Frank Fay as Elwood chattering with Harvey as well as seeing Josephine Hull fluttering through the role of Veta. Their performances did a great deal to help the play become a popular favorite."[15]

Chase acknowledged her indebtedness to Frank Fay's portrayal of Elwood and called it the "best piece of luck."[16] In her modest manner, she told an interviewer, "(Playwriting) is like a party—it's good or bad but you can't quite tell why. I hadn't the faintest idea that *Harvey* would be such a success."[17]

Through the years there have been robust discussions regarding the question of whether the play's messages are of a positive nature or if the play itself dwells too much on the benefits of alcohol.

Frank Fay wholeheartedly disputed the notion that Elwood relies on alcohol for his happiness. "[Harvey] just wants to help a fellow along, that's all. . . . So he appears in various forms to various people. To some he's a weekend vacation; to others he's a blond, to still others he's a bottle of scotch."[18]

Those who object to the way women are portrayed in *Harvey* are most concerned with the abusive behavior that Veta endures and the female stereotypes of Nurse Kelly and Myrtle Mae, who both believe that they need to catch a man.

The dispute on the subject of mental illness centers on both its definition as well as the way to treat it. Chase professed to know little about mental illness, but according to Denver historian Phil Goodstein, she lived near a mental institution and was familiar with a psychiatrist who was attempting to treat patients more humanely.[19]

Drama critic Louis Kronenberger believes the wackiness is a means of conveying "the greatest wisdom and truest happiness."[20] He dismisses the gender tactics as part of the culture of the times.

New York's Roundabout Theatre points to the joy of *Harvey* for telling a sweet, funny, and uplifting tale about a man who tries to be the best person he can be by befriending a six-foot-tall rabbit.[21]

14

A NEW REALITY

On the day after the opening of *Harvey*, the Chases hopped on a train and returned to Denver to try to resume some sort of normality. They heeded the advice of Chase's devoted agent Harold Freedman, a quiet New Yorker who Chase had hired after her initial Broadway debut of *Now You've Done It*, and who was familiar with the rollercoaster rides playwrights often experienced after achieving instant success.

It had been more than two months since the children had seen their mother. Jerry, the youngest, now would not let his mother out of his sight.

The house too had been neglected. Thick layers of dust could be seen everywhere, and every nook and cranny seemed to be somewhat out of place.

After reacquainting herself with her children, Chase focused her attention on her housekeeping chores. She was down in the basement doing laundry when Harold Freedman gave her a call. He wanted to read to her the review by the notable *Nation* critic, Joseph Wood Krutch. Apparently *Harvey* was not just a "smash"; it was a "solid smash." Freedman then explained to her that that meant it was "difficult to buy seats."[1]

The next four years were a bevy of activity and adjustments. The Chases' income level soared to ten times its prior amount. Their lives were constantly under a microscope. Requests poured in for more of Chase's work. Business details needed attention, and Chase's travels were extended. The frazzled playwright struggled to balance all the new elements of her routine. She described it as "clinging to life on a merry-go-round."[2]

MONEY AND FAME

Royalty checks began pouring in. For several years after *Harvey* debuted, Chase's annual income was reported to be one hundred thousand dollars a year.

It was estimated that the income for *Harvey* eventually reached somewhere between eight million and nine million dollars gross.[3]

Overnight, Mary Chase became a household word. She was no longer Li'l Mary, the fun-loving prankster. She was successful Mary Chase whom everyone wanted to meet and either love or hate.

Brock Pemberton called Chase in Denver and urged her to return to New York. "Everybody wants to entertain you."[4] She honored his request but felt terribly uncomfortable in her new role. She felt that when the rich and famous New York crowd met her, they were disappointed.

The phone rang constantly. Strangers knocked at her door. Reporters requested interviews. Producers wanted to buy the rights to her next play. Salesmen and charities wanted her business. Long-lost acquaintances from the past wished to meet her for dinner.

"Darling," said one. "I always knew you could do it. Come to Saturday nite dinner at 8." After twenty-five years of silence, a high school teacher who had disliked Chase in school wrote: "Dearest Mary, I always loved you in your school days and you know that I still do. When can you and I get together?"[5]

Where was the old Mary who read stories to her children, took quiet trips to the grocery store, and invited friends over for her famous lemon meringue pie?

THE WRECKING CREWS

Chase was in shock. She was overwhelmed and became suspicious of everyone. Her old friends stayed away to be respectful and were replaced by strangers approaching her and asking to be friends. She called these people the "wrecking crews" and accused them of being full of greed, envy, and malice.

Her children felt the impact as well. One day Colin came home from school and sought out his mother. "Mom, did you write *Harvey*?" She answered. "Of course I wrote *Harvey*. You watched me write it." Colin answered, "Well, Bud Ferguson says you didn't and even if you did write it, it isn't very good."[6]

Chase was discovering that sudden wealth could bring her physical happiness but neither spiritual nor emotional content. "You expect it to bring you peace of mind," she said. "Instead, it plows up every bit of contentment you ever had."[7]

CONTRACTS AND TOURS

Chase was fortunate to have a devoted agent to handle the efforts involved in keeping three companies going and in handling the long and complicated negotiations for movie rights and overseas production plans. Chase's participation was still required.

Years of commuting began for Chase between New York, Hollywood, Denver, and Europe. She had "speaking acquaintanceships" with celebrities like Tallulah Bankhead and Katharine Cornell, and she dined where all the stars were seen—at Sardi's in New York, Romanoff's in Hollywood, the Ivy in London, and Prunier's in Paris.

BACK TO WORK

It did not take very long after *Harvey* debuted for Chase to be back at work. Within a short period of time she wrote a short story for *McCalls* and transformed her novel *The Banshee* into a play renamed *The Next Half Hour*.

George S. Kaufman, who had written such hits as *You Can't Take It With You* and *Once in a Lifetime* and who had won a Pulitzer Prize for his musical *Of Thee I Sing*, was chosen to direct *The Next Half Hour*. Brock Pemberton thought the time was not right for the play because it was wartime and the play was not upbeat. Instead it was produced by Max Gordon, another respected producer, and starred Fay Bainter, a leading lady who was also a popular film star. It opened at the Empire Theater on October 19, 1945, and closed after eight performances. Neither the critics nor the audience wanted the show to go on.

Chase regretted being talked in to doing the production.

A happier reception came for the short story she wrote for *McCalls* called "He's Our Baby." In the story a teenage boy spreads a rumor about his sister's husband who is a drunkard and has been arrested. All three of them are invited to the home of the brother-in-law's boss, a cranky old woman who gets drunk and gives the sister's husband a promotion despite the rumor. The sister finds out that her brother spread the rumor, but because her husband got a promotion, she decides not to confront her brother about it.

THE HOUSE THAT *HARVEY* BOUGHT

It took only a year after the opening of *Harvey* for the Chase family to move to a mansion in Denver. Chase's agent Harold Freedman assured them that they could afford the sale price of thirty-five thousand dollars. Soon after Mary, Bob, their three children, and Mary's eighty-five-year-old father all moved to 505 Circle Drive in the elegant Country Club neighborhood of Denver. The move took place while Mary was in New York doing rewrites for *The Next Half Hour*.

The arts patron Margery Reed had built the imposing red brick mansion for her sister Mary. It was located next door to Margery Reed's expansive castle. The house stood sternly facing a circular street. It had five adjoining towers decorated on the outside with gingerbread gables, tangled vines, and leaded glass windows.

A big iron gate served as a sentinel to the entrance. Inside a beamed ceiling towered over the living room and was anchored on one end by an extended stone fireplace and on the other by French doors leading out to a garden where a Chinese gazebo, a fish pool with a frog, and a metal sculpture of Pan playing a pipe were placed throughout the yard. Chase's father's suite was on the first floor. Chase's study and library were on the second floor.

Chase now had servants to wash the dishes that before had always been left in her sink. They also did her laundry and made the meals. Everyone was especially happy about someone else doing the cooking because Chase's dishes were always questionable. Said Mary about her new help, "That's what money can buy."[8]

THE FAMILY ADJUSTS

For a while, all three boys remained in Denver and attended the public school near their new home. When Michael graduated from elementary school, he was sent to a boarding school in Connecticut. Both of his brothers also attended the same school after they reached fourteen.

Though she never really explained the reasons why all the boys were sent to private school, based on the circumstances that surrounded this time, it's logical to believe that there were several reasons for the Chases' decision. Above all was Mary's desire to protect her children from all of the intrusions into their private lives once she had become famous. She didn't like her children being bullied or made fun of. It's possible too that Chase might have realized after attending the University of Denver that the opportunities for her children would be greater if they received a more intense, private education. Perhaps Chase had a bit of snobbery in her constitution and liked the idea of joining a more exclusive circle. For certain the Chases now had the financial means to pay for these private schools.

Correspondence from sons Michael and Colin gives some insight into how the children viewed their private school education. Adjusting to the eastern boarding school life was not always easy for any of them. In one of the many letters that Colin writes to his parents, he tells about meeting up with a fellow on the train who feels the same way he does about "Eastern schools." Michael, in one of his letters home, says while he's at school in the east that he longs for his former "easier life."[9]

In the meantime the boys all seemed very happy in their new home. Life was full of friends and fun and some learning. They were just normal kids. They knew their father worked at the *Rocky Mountain News*, and they knew their mother wrote plays. They took it all in stride and just lived their lives.

Many of the boys' friends from that time have spoken nostalgically about all the good times they had at the Chase house. They all loved Chase who could sometimes act more like a kid than they did.

In between her whirlwind life, Chase made sure the boys were well taken care of and she tried as much as she could to have them be a part of her writing life too. When the two older boys were at school in Connecticut, they both joined her in New York to finally see *Harvey*. They were more impressed when they got to see the hit show *Oklahoma* that had premiered the year before *Harvey*.

In 1946, two years after the debut of *Harvey*, the entire Chase family took a two-month hiatus and traveled to Europe. They visited London where Chase was supposed to meet up with Brock Pemberton and make the final plans for a new production company for *Harvey*. Unfortunately Brock Pemberton became ill and could not meet them. With business on the back burner, the Chase family was able to spend more time together visiting the sights of Europe. They attended the best of the London theater circuit and dined with famous London actors and actresses. Bob wrote columns from each of the cities they visited and then sent them back to Denver to be posted in the *News*.

Colin, in particular, loved being a theater critic. After one play the family attended in London, he made a diary entry about one of the actors: "This guy has bad timing. He stinks." Before settling down and becoming a college professor, Colin made several of his own attempts at writing.[10] At one point he thought about writing a book about his mother, but he never did.

The family returned to the United States in April 1947.[11] The boys were happy to be home again and to resume their normal schedules and to go back to their mischievous ways.

Michael's parents insisted that he get a summer job. The other boys were expected to do the same when they became a little older. Chase firmly believed that her children needed to hold jobs in order to learn about life.

Soon after the Chase family returned to America, Chase once more traveled back to London for the opening of *Harvey* at the Birmingham Theatre in London.

Again, there were letters from Bob and the boys. "I miss you, Mom," wrote Colin. "Please come home."[12]

On December 13, 1948, a standing-room-only crowd viewed the opening of *Harvey* starring the English comedian Sid Field as Elwood. Again, the reception was sweeping. After a month in production, the company moved to the Prince of Wales Theatre. Altogether the play ran in London for two years.

HONORS AT HOME

In 1947, three years after its debut on Broadway, after appearing around the country before audiences in New York, Boston, Kansas City, St. Louis, and on the West Coast, and after winning the Pulitzer Prize for Best Drama in 1945, *Harvey* finally came to Colorado. The play was presented at the Central City Opera House outside of Denver where many popular Broadway hits were produced.

Frank Fay re-created his role as Elwood and Marion Lorne, who had taken over the role for Josephine Hull on Broadway, played Veta. Jesse White re-created his original role of Wilson. Brock Pemberton came along for the ride and played Elwood one night even though Chase was never smitten whenever he decided to play the part. She thought he was too old. Once again, *Harvey* was a hit. The play enjoyed a run of thirty-three performances, the maximum number allotted to the summer theater's limited residence.

When interviewed by the *News* at the time, Chase was asked how she felt about *Harvey* making an appearance in Denver. Chase expressed great delight. "I feel that *Harvey* has come back home. The play started here and I always wanted Denver people to see it."[13]

In her typical Mary Chase style, she never expressed a trace of bitterness that Denver gave her *Harvey* and her other successful plays a less than welcoming reception. In her lifetime two limited productions of *Harvey*, both benefits, and one of *Lolita* for a children's theater conference were produced briefly at the Bonfils Theater that began in 1953. Other productions of Chase's plays were presented at surrounding regional theaters including Elitch's, Central City, the Country Dinner Playhouse, the Changing Scene Theater, and the University of Denver.

When Helen Bonfils, the daughter of Frederick Bonfils, the publisher of the *Denver Post* and the heir to the Bonfils estate, originated her theater in 1953, it had been forty years since Denver had had a professional theater. A passionate advocate for the arts, Miss Helen, as she was called because she never married until later in life, felt that the increasing popularity of the University Civic Theater did not allow for growth. Beginning in 1940, she began to make plans to build a larger theater. After her initial purchase of land proved to be ineffective, she donated the property to the university and bought another property on East Colfax and Elizabeth a few miles from downtown Denver. It was an extravagant facility that took several years to complete. The grand opening took place in 1953 with a production of the play *Green Grow the Lilacs*. A year after the Denver Civic Theatre opened, the name was changed to the Bonfils Theatre in Miss Helen's honor and Denver Civic Theatre was used to describe the name of the resident company.

Helen Bonfils was a passionate proponent of Denver theater, and her achievements remain in high esteem among city founders. With her resources and influence, she was able to make great progress in establishing a vibrant theater climate. She was not an innovator or willing to take risks. The plays that were produced at the Bonfils always had a track record. Perhaps that is one of the reasons why Mary Chase's plays were not selected.

In 1978 the Bonfils Theatre was absorbed into the Denver Center for the Performing Arts complex that was built after Bonfils died in 1972. No production of any of Chase's plays has ever been presented at the Denver Center for the Performing Arts.

After *Harvey*'s run on Broadway, Chase did enjoy some local recognition. The Colorado Authors' League presented her with its William McCleod Reine Award in 1944 and the University of Denver conferred on her an honorary doctorate of letters in 1947. She also enjoyed an enthusiastic reception when she spoke at a University of Denver Writers' Workshop in 1947. Her continued association with the University of Denver where she had spent two years of her college life influenced her decision to donate the original *Harvey* manuscript to the University of Denver Library in 1963.

15

THE PULITZER PRIZE

MARY WINS THE PULITZER

In May of 1945 Chase was at a movie theater with a friend watching the film version of *You Can't Take It With You* when Bob called her out of the theater to tell her that *Harvey* had won the 1945 Pulitzer Prize for Drama. He was at work and had just read the news over the Associated Press wire.

"I just yelled when he told me. I had wanted to win the Pulitzer Prize all my life . . . and I had no idea I'd ever get it."[1]

The announcement read: "*Harvey* by Mary Chase. For the original American play, performed in New York, which shall best represent in marked fashion the educational value and power of the stage, preferably dealing with American life."[2] Chase also received a financial reward of five hundred dollars.

THE DECISION

The members of the 1945 Pulitzer Prize jury had hardly any problem at all in agreeing on a favorite play for the year. Along with *Harvey* by Mary Chase, they had conducted exhaustive discussions about the other candidates: *Dark of the Moon* by Howard Richardson and William Berney as well as *The Hasty Heart* by John Patrick and a last minute entry, *The Glass Menagerie*, by the young playwright Tennessee Williams. *Harvey* was the unanimous choice "on account of its richness of content and the fresh imaginative field it had taken over; as well as in plot and character that marked a departure from the usual Broadway play."[3]

The jury had delayed its decision until one member could see the play by Williams. When there was no objection after he had seen the play, the award was unanimously conferred on *Harvey*. The decision created quite a stir among some critics who felt *Glass Menagerie* should have been the winner. Many felt that the choice of *Harvey* was not in keeping with the highest morals because Elwood was presented as a lush, but John Hohenberg, who at the time had been the award's administrator for twenty years, made no apologies for the selection. *Harvey* was just what Americans needed and wanted: "Laughter and relief from anxiety in the closing months of World War II."[4]

THE CONTROVERSY

If judgment is made solely on the basis of popularity, *Harvey* is the undisputed winner. The total number of performances for *Harvey* was 1,775; for *The Glass Menagerie* the number was 561.

Controversy occurred because some critics felt that *The Glass Menagerie* explored more deeply its themes and values. Other critics questioned whether a story about an amiable but tipsy man was of educational value.

Critic John Toohey offered his explanation for his opposition to the Pulitzer Prize choice:

> It is difficult to understand how Williams' first masterpiece, *The Glass Menagerie* blessed with the magnificent performance of Laurette Taylor, failed to impress the Pulitzer jurors or the advisory board. Not awarding the prize to Williams represents possibly the biggest error the Pulitzer committee has made in its assessment in any theater season. The whimsy of a drunkard who hallucinates a six-foot tall rabbit simply cannot compare in dramatic value to the passionate, fully realized portrait of American life that Williams presented in his great memory play, *The Glass Menagerie.*[5]

The Drama Critics' Circle, the other professional organization whose jury was composed of all critics, chose *The Glass Menagerie* as the "best play written by an American playwright and produced in New York."[6]

In regard to the implications that Elwood was a lush who saw the pooka because he drank, Chase adamantly defended her work. "It's not a play about a drunk," she insisted. "Elwood would see Harvey anyway. The liquor was inserted to keep it from being a preachment."[7]

Tennessee Williams later won Pulitzer Prizes in 1948 for *Streetcar Named Desire* and in 1955 for *Cat on a Hot Tin Roof.*

THE THEATER AWARDS

As the world has expanded in population, so too has the number of organizations that mete out theater awards. Each organization uses different criteria for their decisions. Must they be original works, or can they be revivals? Should they be produced on Broadway, or can they be produced Off-Broadway or elsewhere in the country? Can they include musicals? Is an American theme of importance? The undisputed belief of almost everyone in the theatrical world is that to win any of these awards is an honor and many times a life changer.

The Pulitzer Prize for Drama began in 1918. The movement for the award had its start much earlier in 1904 when journalism magnate Joseph Pulitzer approached Columbia University to create awards to serve as an incentive for excellence and as an alternative to the Swedish Nobel Prize. He wanted to cover the fields of journalism, letters, drama, and education. In addition, the Pulitzer board was charged with awarding five traveling scholarships. By the time the Pulitzer Prizes were established, Joseph Pulitzer had passed away.

To determine the award, it was decided that a jury, made up of one academic and four critics, attend plays in New York and in regional theaters. The Pulitzer board had the authority to overrule the jury's choice, however. Later the jury's number was extended to seven and included representation by a playwright.

Controversy had beset the Pulitzer Prize in the past. In 1936 critics had been extremely disturbed that the Pulitzer Prize was given to Robert E. Sherwood for his play *Idiot's Delight* rather than to Lillian Hellman for *The Children's Hour* that dealt with the questionable relationship of two female schoolteachers. In response the critics organized the Drama Critics' Circle award with a jury made up entirely of drama critics. The group determined their criteria for an award to be "the best play written by an American playwright and produced in New York."[8]

According to theater expert Paul Firestone, the difference between the Pulitzer Prize and the Drama Critics' Circle Award is that the Pulitzer committee picks a play that is the best theater for our American democracy and the Drama Critics' Circle pick a play that is the best theater in absolute terms. The two groups have agreed on the same play twenty-five times out of the eighty years they have been coexisting.[9]

Even though Chase lost out to Williams in the category of best play, Drama Critics' Circle did award Josephine Hull the award for Best Supporting Actress and Frank Fay won for Best Actor. Years later, Chase's play *Mrs. McThing* was a runner-up for the Drama Critics' Circle Award for best play.

In 1947, three years after *Harvey* made its Broadway premiere, the awards scene expanded even further with the establishment of the Tony Awards by The

American Theatre Wing in memory of Antoinette Perry for her contributions to the American theater. The Tony has become the benchmark for excellence in theater. The awards are chosen by a committee of twenty-four who represent all of the participants necessary to produce a play on Broadway including playwrights, producers, directors, actors, designers, choreographers, and technicians. When a revival of *Harvey* appeared on Broadway in 1972, the esteemed actress Helen Hayes won a Tony for Best Supporting Actress and Jimmy Stewart received a nomination for Best Actor. Jose Ferrer won over Stewart for his performance in *Cyrano de Bergerac*. Because *Harvey* was a revival, no award for best playwright could be considered.

In addition to the Pulitzer, the Drama Critics' Circle Award, and the Tony, the Drama Desk Awards was established in 1955 to recognize excellence in New York theater productions Off-Broadway as well as on-Broadway productions. More and more theater organizations continue to evolve and create more opportunities for those in the world of theater.

Said Paul Firestone, "It is difficult, if not impossible, to say whose selections have been the superior. But it seems that honoring more plays encourages more theatergoing and spurs American playwrights to greater productivity."[10]

THE EXCLUSIVE CLUB

When Chase was chosen as a Pulitzer Prize winner for drama, she entered an exclusive circle. Many of her successors and predecessors were playwrights that she revered and admired and are still held in high esteem. Some of those playwrights working at the same time as Chase and who received Best Drama awards before and after are Eugene O'Neill (*Strange Interlude*, 1928), Thornton Wilder (*Our Town*, 1939), William Saroyan (*The Time of Our Life*, 1940), Arthur Miller (*Death of a Salesman*, 1949), and Tennessee Williams (*Streetcar Named Desire*, 1948).

Mary Chase was the first person from Colorado to win a Pulitzer Prize for Drama. She continues to be the only Colorado recipient.

WOMEN PULITZER PLAYWRIGHTS

When Chase received the Pulitzer Prize, she was only the fourth woman to do so since the inception of the Pulitzer Prize in 1918. One hundred years after the birth of the Pulitzer Prize for Drama, only fourteen women have received the award.

After Chase's success, it would be thirteen more years before another woman received the best drama award in 1958 and then another twenty-three years before it happened again.

Mary Chase had been preparing herself for serious playwriting since she was eleven and fell in love with the theater. She gave a share of the credit to her husband and called him her Rock of Gibralter.

"The Pulitzer Prize should come in two sections," she said, "one for the winner and one for the winner's mate."[11]

Receiving the Pulitzer Prize confirmed to Chase that others recognized her as a respected and legitimate playwright. What would she do next to keep the momentum going?

16

HOLLYWOOD

THE MILLION-DOLLAR DEAL

A few months before Chase received the Pulitzer Prize in October 1945, she had some other good news. RKO Universal International Pictures wanted to make a movie of *Harvey* and pay her a million dollars for the rights to produce it. At the time, it was the most amount of money that had ever been offered a playwright for movie rights.

In her usual understated style, Chase seemed less interested in the money than she was in making sure that the movie was done well. Her contract stipulated that she had complete control over the casting of the movie. The making of the movie was delayed until the Broadway run had finished, which did not take place until 1949.

Henry Koster, a seasoned director who had escaped from Germany in 1936, was chosen to direct. Oscar Brodney, a successful screenwriter of the time, was hired to help Chase write the screenplay.

Mary Chase and Brock Pemberton were each to receive one hundred thousand dollars per year for ten years against one-third of the film's profits. Pemberton died in March of 1950, before the start of the production.

JIMMY STEWART AND ELWOOD

Just as selecting an actor to play Elwood for the play production was a challenge, finding the right actor for the film again proved to be time-consuming. Among the actors considered were Bing Crosby, Cary Grant, Rudy Vallee, Joe E. Brown,

Gary Cooper, Jack Benny, Jack Haley, and James Cagney. Even Harold Lloyd, who had turned down the role on Broadway, was interested. It was thought that Frank Fay did not have enough national name recognition to be considered. One more name was under consideration: Jimmy Stewart, who had already substituted twice for Fay on Broadway and whose appearances had been well received.

The part was first offered to Bing Crosby who accepted and then reneged when his agent suggested to him that his following might not like to see him play an inebriated gentleman after his recent performance as a priest in *Going My Way* (1944).

Jimmy Stewart really wanted the role, but Universal wanted him for *Winchester '73*, another film the company was currently producing. A deal was made that Stewart could do *Harvey* if he promised to do *Winchester '73* too.

Many of the original cast members were hired to re-create their Broadway roles. Josephine Hull again played Veta and Jesse White again reenacted Wilson, the sanitarium attendant.

Stewart got another bonus when *Winchester '73* (a film he only agreed to do in order to win the lead in *Harvey*) became an even bigger hit and encouraged him to play tougher, more complex characters in 1950s action films.

Jimmy Stewart always said that *Harvey* was his favorite role.

MARY ON SET

The production was filmed at Universal Studios in California from April to June in 1950 with Chase in attendance.

In contrast to the original stage play that had two sets, the Dowd library and the reception room at Chumley's Rest, more than twenty scenes were filmed on the lot of Universal Studios. Among the sets were the sidewalk in front of the Dowd mansion, the garden where Dr. Chumley grew his precious dahlias at the entrance to Chumley's Rest, and Charlie's bar where Elwood and Harvey meet Dr. Sanderson and Nurse Kelly. "We wanted to get the visual effects just as much as we wanted that lovely dialogue," said Koster.[1]

Henry Koster kept the script of the film as close to the original play as possible with Chase writing only a limited amount of additional dialogue that Koster explained had to be done "for cinematic purposes."[2]

A significant addition was the widening of the screen to allow the invisible Harvey to have more room for his "appearance."

Other technical changes were also addressed. Jimmy Stewart was six feet, four inches tall so the height of Harvey was extended from six-foot, one-and-a-half inches in the play to six-foot, three inches in the movie.

Due to regulations at the time, the Hollywood Hays Code did not allow the filming of the consumption of alcohol. Instead Elwood was filmed ordering drinks at the bar.

Again Mary Chase wanted the film audience to actually see Harvey at the end because she "didn't want anybody to go out of the theater thinking Elwood is just a lush. He believes in Harvey . . . and I think the audience ought to believe in Harvey, too."[3] The studio reportedly considered this and experimented with how to show him to the audience, including his appearance in silhouette, and even by attaching a rabbit tail to the taxi driver at the film's conclusion but all of these ideas were eventually rejected. Reminded by Brock Pemberton of the disastrous results of introducing a live Harvey in the Boston tryout of 1944, the decision was made to keep a real Harvey off the screen. When the end credits run over photographs of the actors, Harvey's credit is imposed over an unattended door opening and closing.

Shooting the film was quick and pleasant for all. "I must say it was a complete, one hundred percent pleasure, the whole picture," said Henry Koster. "I had the most wonderful performers. The spirit of Harvey, that splendid and helpful ghost, was always with us while we did it."[4] In fact, as a joke, the cast and crew of *Harvey* often set a chair for the title character at lunch and ordered him something to eat.

Those who were on the set recall the filming as a very pleasant experience.

Jimmy Stewart had many kind things to say about Chase. At his 1978 surprise appearance in Denver for Harvey's thirty-fifth anniversary, he said, "Knowing Mary Chase has been a wonderful experience for me. She always fought for me and gave me encouragement."[5]

Henry Koster said that Chase was a "very nice lady to work with and a great writer of comedy."[6]

Chase said she didn't stay around the set more than she had to. She thought the movie was "never as good a movie as it was a stage play."[7] She felt it was more difficult to create a sense of mystery and anticipation in a two-dimensional film. She also thought that Jimmy Stewart was too young to play the part of Elwood.

THE FILM (1950)

Harvey premiered in New York in December of 1950. The movie received two Golden Globe nominations for Best Actress in a Supporting Role (Josephine Hull) and Best Actor (James Stewart). Hull won in her category, but Stewart lost to Jose Ferrer for his role of Cyrano de Bergerac. Best picture went to Billy Wilder's *Sunset Boulevard* starring William Holden and Gloria Swanson.

Josephine Hull won the Academy Award for best supporting actress. Jimmy Stewart was nominated for best actor but again lost to Jose Ferrer for his role as Cyrano de Bergerac. Best picture went to *All About Eve* starring Bette Davis. Neither the Hollywood Foreign Press nor the Academy of Motion Picture Arts and Sciences nominated *Harvey* for best screenplay.

Even though the reviews were positive, Universal failed to reach its financial goals until much later. In 1990 *Harvey* was released on VHS and introduced by Jimmy Stewart. The video continues to be a best seller and helped Universal recover its losses.

"Stewart and his bunny buddy turned *Harvey* into 14 carrot gold."[8]

Mary Coyle Chase's Denver home from 1907 to 1931.

A "Li'l Mary and Charlie" column entry for the *Rocky Mountain News*, circa 1928. Text by Mary Coyle. Illustration by Charlie Wunder.

Rocky Mountain News reporter Mary Chase and photographer Harry
Rhoads having fun, circa 1929.

Antoinette Perry, the co-producer and director of *Harvey*, circa 1944.
MSThr 382 (318).

A real Harvey and Mary Chase at the Boston tryout of *Harvey* in 1946.

Frank Fay, Mary Chase, and Brock Pemberton prepare for the 1947 Central City, Colorado, production of *Harvey*.

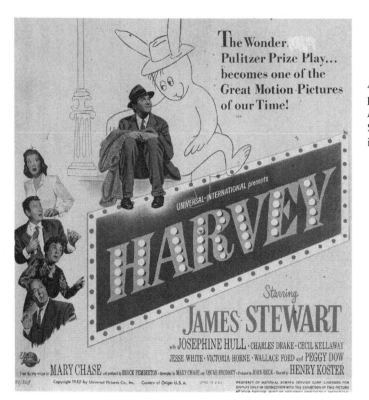

A window card promotes the movie *Harvey* starring Jimmy Stewart that debuted in 1950.

"Mary Chase Alley," New York, 1952.

Mary Chase and Joe, the family springer spaniel, circa 1952.

Harold Berson's cover illustration of *Loretta Mason Potts* by Mary Chase.

Comedian Joe E. Brown and University President Campton Bell surround Mary Chase as she donates the original *Harvey* manuscript to the University of Denver in 1963.

Robert Chase, husband of Mary Chase, is greeted by the Secretary of Navy in Hawaii, 1957.

Robert and Mary Chase with group on naval ship, 1957.

Michael and Colin Chase and their wives attend a performance of *Harvey* at Central City, Colorado, in 1971.

Mary Chase in her study at the
"House That Harvey Bought."

Jimmy Stewart and Mary
Chase together in Denver
at the 35th anniversary
of *Harvey*.

ACT III

After *Harvey*

Mary Chase was thirty-seven years old when she became a highly regarded and successful playwright. Her husband was already part of the hierarchy at the *Rocky Mountain News*, and her children were twelve, ten, and nine years of age.

If she had wanted to keep her reputation as a "housewife who wrote plays," she could easily have rested on her laurels and gone back to raising her children, making lemon meringue pies, and helping others.

What prevented her from this choice was a combination of the demands that come with fame, her own personal need for continued self-fulfillment, and a hidden desire to surpass the success she had achieved with *Harvey*.

17

SETTLING DOWN

CONQUERING THE WHISKEY AND SODA ROUTE

Brock Pemberton said a hit is always a traumatic thing for playwrights. He said most follow the whiskey and soda route, but a few are smart enough to go back to work. Chase did both.[1]

Chase was aware of her increasing attachment to alcohol and worked hard to get her problem under control. Though it is not clear how she learned to combat her dependency, the results were evident and positive. Instead of reaching for a drink, she began to exercise, establish a regular daily routine, and rely on her church for support. Having long ago abandoned the Catholic Church, Chase had settled on attending the First Church of Christ of Science, a church that matched her more secular and spiritual inclinations. In addition, it became a mission of hers to help other women who were less fortunate than she learn to curb their addictive tendencies.

THE ROUTINE

A rigid routine helped Chase return to sobriety.

Each day she buried herself in the spare second story unheated room of her new home and pounded away on her typewriter for anywhere from five to twelve hours. She called the room her "prison." Sometimes she worked away on new projects. At other times she returned to prior scripts.

Every day she rose at seven, read several passages in her Bible, took a brisk forty-five minute walk before coming home to ring for breakfast, a healthy one of boiled eggs, toast, and coffee, which she ate while reading the newspaper. By nine o'clock she was at work. She sat at a hard chair facing a small table that supported her typewriter. A narrow bed nearby was used as a catchall for reams of typing paper, boxes of envelopes, pencils, and scribbled notes.

Normally around two in the afternoon after endless cigarettes and cups of coffee, she emerged from her prison and entered her library next door, warmly furnished with easy chairs and a couch set before a fireplace. Over a newly brewed pot of coffee brought in by a maid, she learned of telephone calls received during the morning and then returned them at once.

Skipping lunch in an effort to watch her figure, Chase then prepared for the afternoon when she would dress up to greet her visitors. She donned a stylish afternoon dress and always embellished it with jewelry. When friends came to call, another fresh pot of coffee was served. Occasionally her visitors would stay for dinner that was served promptly at 6:30 p.m. to please Bob. Until her father passed away in 1954, Frank joined them for dinner and lent his Irish humor to those at the table. By eleven o'clock all lights in the Chase house were usually out.[2]

HOUSE OF HOPE

In the early 1950s Chase and some of her friends organized a charity that they called the House of Hope. They went to work to fund a facility where women who were suffering from alcoholism and did not have the means to pay for treatment could live and be helped.

To pay for the beginning costs of the organization, Chase convinced comedian Joe E. Brown, who played Elwood in the touring company of *Harvey*, to come to Denver and present a shortened production of *Harvey*. The touring company had just completed their run, and Brown graciously agreed to headline their event. Chase's friend Margaret Perry Fanning, daughter of Antoinette Perry, acted in the production. Denver society attended and the event raised ten thousand dollars.

A ribbon cutting ceremony for the facility took place the following spring. Years later the House of Hope was absorbed into a facility at nearby Fort Logan Hospital. Though Chase was involved in the whole process, her name is never mentioned in the publicity. She was to say later that one of her greatest sources of pride was helping to found the House of Hope.

REAPING THE REWARDS

Chase rarely had a problem spending money. Once she could spend it more freely she continued to indulge in the ways she had always done even when the bills kept coming in before *Harvey*.

She had always had a passion for hats and clothes, but now she could explore the shops in New York, London, and Paris as well and take a look at what the designers had to offer. Eventually she bought herself a mink coat, an ermine wrap, and a few coats trimmed with collars of sable and other luxurious furs.

Michael, the oldest son who, like his mother, enjoyed the finer things in life, did complain once in a letter to her when she bought herself a mink coat and not a car for him, but in the same letter he forgave her. "A family," he said, "is a wonderful thing. I mean it's one group that is on your side regardless."[3]

Her expanded new home gave her rooms to decorate with Chinese art and antiques, and she regularly searched for items to place in the dollhouses she collected. A Cadillac replaced the family Ford.

When they finally had some time and even more of a windfall from Mary's new concurrent plays on Broadway, Bob and Mary Chase spent some time traveling.

In 1953 they were off to Italy and France on the *Mauretania*, whose list of passengers included George Burns, the well-known television and radio personality.

In 1956 they took a first-class cruise around the world. The fifty-eight-day trip aboard the SS *Constitution* took them to cities in Europe, the Middle East, and Africa. In the company of prominent leaders of both Colorado and other parts of the United States, they ate more than three thousand meals on board the ship. Bob chronicled the trip with articles he wrote and then submitted to the *News*, among them "The Road to Damascus" and "Barbed Wire Around Jerusalem."

The next year the Chases were off to the South Pacific where Bob, now an associate editor of the *News*, was a guest of the Navy in Hawaii. The couple then continued on to take another cruise, this time to Samoa, Fiji, Tahiti, Australia, and New Zealand. Photographs in Bob's scrapbook depict Bob and his wife elegantly dressed and dining at a table for eight. Chase is wearing a strapless floral dress, donning her ermine stole, and looking quite ravishing with her hair piled high on her head. She seldom smiles in any of her pictures, and neither does Bob, but it's hard to think that they weren't enjoying themselves.

Bob and Mary Chase took one more cruise to the West Indies in 1959 and then stopped traveling. That cruise went to Jamaica, the Caribbean Islands, and Havana. A photo of some of the women on board the trip with Mary shows them all in printed sundresses with a backdrop of sun, sand, and palm trees.

Chase generously shared her new wealth with family members. She bought houses for her brother Charlie who lived in California and one in Denver for her husband's mother.

Throughout her life she donated to charities she supported, especially if they were related to the theater.

SHE'S STILL MARY

After *Harvey*, Chase did become more subdued but that edgy humor of hers still could surface. Once she embarrassed her agent, a shy, humble man, by screaming across the room to him at Sardi's restaurant. Another time on an elevator she assumed a fake New York accent and berated her friend Margaret Perry Fanning when Fanning began to stroke the fur on Chase's coat. Often she amused herself by using the wrong names to introduce people to each other.

Between her children, her husband, and herself, 505 was always bustling with characters streaming in and out. She renewed her old friendships and constantly acquired new ones.

Visitors continued to represent a cross-section of social and economic life. She particularly enjoyed hosting teas for friends. "I loved the tea she gave for me when I was getting married," recalled Susan Hilb whose mother-in-law, Greta, a respected artist in the community, was good friends with Chase. Hilb cites some of the women who were present including Frances Melrose, a reporter at the *Rocky Mountain News*, and Leonora Mattingly Weber, a writer of popular teenage novels. Hilb recalls that Chase served alcohol and she felt very grown up.[4]

Throughout her life, there were always notes of encouragement to be written to friends far and near and observations on politics and life in general to be made. Though some observers noted a certain sense of melancholy in Chase's persona, it did not keep her from staying in touch with an interesting and wide circle of family and friends.

At this point in her life Mary had learned to control the disruptions that were now a recognized fact of life and to accept human nature's flaws. She is famous for saying "Man is truly a magnificent creature badly dressed sometimes."[5]

18

NEW BEGINNINGS

The time after Chase's return from London proved to be one of her most productive writing periods. She began working on two plays that made it to Broadway, *Mrs. McThing* and *Bernardine*. Several other ideas were tossed around and, though unfinished, were addressed from time to time during her daily writing regimen.

During this period her children were at school in the east. Jerry and Colin were in Connecticut. Colin, after graduation, moved on to a seminary in Missouri. Michael began college in Pennsylvania and soon after moved to Virginia to launch his career in theater. When the boys returned home for holidays, Chase put her writing on hold so she could enjoy being with them and their legions of friends.

After months of silence Chase welcomed the activity of her brood. The record player blared, and she ordered her staff to keep replenishing the refrigerator. She wanted to be with them as much as she could.

Bob was now working days as associate editor of the *News*. Whenever Mary took on a new writing project, he just said "Oh God" and kept on working.

THE WORK GOES ON

Before her simultaneous successes, Chase struggled to find her compass. In 1949 she tried again to write a serious play. She called it *The Snow Queen*. She wanted to show what her life had been like as a society reporter in the 1920s. It took place in an elegant mansion in Snowcrest, Colorado, where socialites circulated with the intent of catching the eye of Miss Dacey, the society editor of the local newspaper. She shows how precarious a society reporter's position can be when

Miss Dacey loses her job to an apprentice for printing a wrong name. The play ends happily though when she gets her job back. *The Snow Queen* was never published or produced.

MARY CHASE ALLEY

In 1952, within six months of one another, two new and successful Mary Chase plays, *Mrs. McThing* and *Bernardine*, premiered on Broadway and enjoyed decent Broadway runs. So impressed were the Broadway scions that they temporarily changed the name of Shubert Alley, the famous Broadway side street, to "Mary Chase Alley."

Chase's magic with her plays was definitely translating into financial rewards. She was earning a thousand dollars a week for *Mrs. McThing* and two thousand dollars a week for *Bernardine* in addition to all her other profits that she continued to receive for *Harvey*.[1]

Drama critics and reviewers were amazed at her success. She had consistently toughened Broadwayites. She didn't write plays for money like normal people, and her plays were never considered "normal." Said one crotchety producer, "And what's the point? The point is the public loves her screwy off-beat shows."[2]

An Associated Press writer commented: "One of the astounding aspects of dramatist Mary Chase's career is her complete lack of any resemblance of the popular stereotype of a Broadway playwright. . . . (She) never pretends to be anything more than a wife and mother who writes plays in her spare time."[3]

BLESS THE CHILDREN

While *Harvey* was still in production, the actress Ina Claire, after she had seen the play, suggested to Chase that she might want to write a play for children. She thought children needed to use their imaginations more fully, and if an adult play like *Harvey* could provide some magic, why couldn't a play for children do the same? Chase concurred. She too felt that no dramatist had satisfied a youngster's hunger for the magical world of theater since J. M. Barrie had written *Peter Pan*. When Chase mentioned the idea to Antoinette Perry, Perry was skeptical. She felt it would be difficult not to talk down to children.

Soon after her conversation with Claire, Chase observed the English approach to children's theater when she was visiting there for the London opening production of *Harvey*. From that point on, it became a passion of hers to write for children that lasted throughout the remainder of her life. She was impressed with how early the English introduced their young ones to the theater, and she loved the pantomimes and puppetry they used to entice them. She thought the stage could engage the young in ways that could not be done with the two-dimensional presentations of superheroes and fairytales they saw in the movies. Television at the time was not yet widely in use, but she probably would have also applied her observation to that medium as it too was two-dimensional and not interactive.[4]

MR. OR MRS. McTHING?

Chase began writing *Mrs. McThing* immediately after her return from London, but she did not share her idea with anyone. She was still superstitious about such things.

She decided to aim her play at an audience of youngsters between seven and fourteen. Her sons were ten, eleven, and fourteen at the time she began to write the play.

The idea for *Mrs. McThing* came from a childhood memory about a changeling, a character in Irish lore who turns someone who behaves badly into a different person. In the play, young Howay, the son of a rich widow, lives a lonely, isolated life in a mansion and is befriended by a young girl named Mimi whose mother is a witch. Mimi's mother, the changeling, arranges an exchange of Howay for a "stick," a well-behaved son longed for by Howay's mother. The mother tires of the well-behaved son and goes searching for the real Howay and is forced to dirty her hands by becoming a part of a working-class environment. All ends well when Howay's mother is able to retrieve her son and welcome Howay's new friends into her widened circle.

Chase corralled her son Jerry, now twelve, and his pals to come and listen to the play. The other boys were already attending school in the east. Chase was a big believer in reading her plays to everyday people. This was always a practice of hers. She was looking for her audience's reactions. She knew that if her audience started scraping their chairs or shifting their positions, she was not keeping them interested.

"She bribed us," recalled Jerry's friend Tom Hilb. "She told us she'd feed us hot dogs and ice cream if we would listen to her read her play."[5] Hilb remembered the ice cream more than the play.

The readings were done several times, and when Chase asked the boys for feedback, they wanted to know why there were no gangsters. Movies at the time were full of gangsters and so were articles in the local newspapers.

Gangsters with names like Poison Eddie and Stinker were then added to Chase's script. Chase also discovered that pure comedy alone did not work on a young audience. The antics could not be subtle. They had to be more slapstick if they were to keep the audience interested. There had to be more chases, more boxing, and more falls. Surprisingly her audience insisted on the need to face the fact that there was sadness in the world. In other words, the play had to have a message.

The original draft was completed by 1949. It was copyrighted as *Mr. Thing* because the witch at that time was a male warlock.

In 1951 Chase submitted *Mr. Thing* to the Barter Theatre in Abingdon, Virginia, for production. Her son Michael was beginning his theatrical career with the company and was working as an intern. The Barter began in 1933 and was the country's first professional regional theater.

It didn't take long for Broadway producers to catch wind of the production of Chase's new play. They began to persistently court her to bring *Mr. Thing* to Broadway. Chase rejected their offers. She did not want to present the play to a Broadway audience. The play, she insisted, was only for kids.

Chase's rejections did not keep her agent Harold Freedman and Robert Whitehead, a preeminent producer who was the president of the American National Theater Academy, from paying a visit to Chase in Denver to try to convince her to allow *Mr. Thing* to be produced on Broadway. "Mary," urged Whitehead, "half the world is adult."[6]

The reluctant Mary Chase finally gave in, but she stipulated that she only wanted the play to have a limited three-week run. Soon after *Mr. Thing* became *Mrs. McThing*, a menacing female witch.

Helen Hayes, the highly respected actress, was president of the American National Theater Academy at the time and was cast as Mrs. Howard LaRue, the wealthy dowager mother. Said Hayes, "I fell in love with *Mrs. McThing* as soon as I read the script."[7]

Howay was played by thirteen-year-old Brandon DeWilde who had just starred in the Broadway hit of *Member of the Wedding* and later became a popular screen star after his movie debut in *Shane*.

The cast also included the debut of Fred Gwynne, the future leading actor in the popular television series *The Munsters*. Jules Munshin, a well-known comedic actor, was also a member of the cast.

Directing *Mrs. McThing* was Joseph Buloff who had directed the award-winning musical *Oklahoma* two years before.

A successful tryout took place in February 1952 at the Parsons Theatre in Hartford before it made its way to Broadway. Four additional nights were added on to the original run.

Mrs. McThing was presented by the American National Theatre Academy at the Martin Beck Theatre on February 20, 1952. As Chase had specified, the play was scheduled to run for three weeks.

Instead the play continued for a year and ran for 350 performances, surprising everyone. Ms. Hayes commented about the extension, "Such fun to be stuck with."[8]

Critics said that the Helen Hayes role was "a perfect blend of fantasy and reality."[9]

Said Hayes, "I think Mrs. Chase (did) such a wise and witty job of creating the point of view of the child and showing the world very simply and logically as a child sees it."[10]

Mrs. McThing captured the approval of many New York critics. Brooks Atkinson of the *New York Times* was indebted to Ireland for "Mrs. Chase's rich make-believe sense of humor and her compassion for the needs of adults and children." Comparing *Mrs. McThing* to *Harvey*, he believed that it was "a richer play with a broader point of view, a greater area of compassion, and a more innocent sense of comedy."[11]

Richard Watts in a *New York Post* article made positive comparisons of *Mrs. McThing* to *Peter Pan* and indicated that both protagonists flee homes in revolt against parental stiffness and that both plays had gangsters that are amusing and incompetent.[12]

When the play was presented in London in 1956, the critics didn't care for the permissiveness of *Mrs. McThing*. In countering the English assessment, one observer remarked that "*Mrs. McThing* is uniquely American," and that instead of being a European fairytale, Howay is rich rather than royal.[13]

In a "My Day" column, Eleanor Roosevelt lauded the play. "Who among us, when we were young, didn't live a hundred different lives and impersonate a hundred different people in our day dreams? These day dreams are the basis for *Mrs. McThing*."[14]

Jerry Chase and his friends could take great pride in the final product. There were gangsters, funny business, and there was a deep message, a "heart-line," that the greatest force is still a mother's love. As Mrs. LaRue says, "I love my son, but I do most of the wrong things mothers do."[15]

Mrs. McThing was runner up for the Drama Critics' Circle for best play for 1951/1952. John Van Druten won for *I Am A Camera*. But John Chapman, the *New York Daily News* drama critic, contested the decision. His personal choice for the best play of the year was Mary Chase's *Mrs. McThing*, "a sweet and skillful fantasy."[16]

The following summer the Broadway Company took a break to perform near Denver at the Central City Opera House. By that time Chase and Helen Hayes had struck up a friendship that would continue throughout Chase's lifetime. They had great fun together in Colorado. While Hayes was appearing in *Mrs. McThing* at Central City, she and her husband, Charles MacArthur, were celebrating their twenty-fifth wedding anniversary. To honor the occasion, Chase presented them with a medal award made from a Colorado silver mine. Bob and Mary Chase later visited the MacArthurs at their home in upstate New York, and Chase and Hayes enjoyed a correspondence and a relationship until Chase passed away in 1981. When Jimmy Stewart and Hayes starred in a revival of *Harvey* on Broadway in 1970, Chase and Stewart renewed their friendship. Stewart, Hayes, and Chase became lifelong friends. They all shared the same outlook on life. They were down-to-earth people who had an appreciation for the masses.

The popularity of *Mrs. McThing* spread quickly. An excerpt of the play with the witches appeared on television's *The Ed Sullivan Show*, and a several page pictorial spread was published in *Life Magazine*. *Mrs. McThing* proved that a play could be both a financial and artistic success.

Mrs. McThing remains a frequent choice for high school productions. The author of this book was a member of her high school stage crew for a production of *Mrs. McThing* in the late 1950s.

BERNARDINE ON STAGE AND SCREEN

Chase had simultaneously been busy at work on another play with Irving Jacobs, a Denver resident directing the play. When Jacobs died, New York director Guthrie McClintic took over the task.

Using her three sons for inspiration, Chase wrote *Bernardine* about eight high school youths from Sneaky Falls, Idaho, who hang around together at a local beer parlor, called Shamrock Snooze patterned after the Eastway, a real hangout that her uncles often visited in early twentieth-century Denver.[17] There they spend time playing practical jokes on Wormy Weldy, a nerdy fellow, and where they dream endlessly about the perfect woman who will always say yes to their advances. Their leader, Beau, dreams up a scheme to have the ideal woman, Bernardine (the name of a Franciscan saint who can be male or female), call them up on the phone and woo them. The opening of the play begins with a soliloquy by Beau in a style resembling that of the stage manager in *Our Town* (1938) and foreshadows the actions that take place:

> It is a Hallowe'en world they (teenage boys) live in for a little while and their light heartedness comes, I believe, from the fact that as they stand on the top of the hill, as it were and look at the Earth beneath, they do not quite believe in it; so they give off with a Bronx cheer and with an index finger draw crazy circles in the sky—blending skyscrapers and grapefruit rinds, bankers and bebop in a Daliesque signature. They own nothing of it and so they own it all.[18]

Bernardine debuted on Broadway at the Playhouse Theatre on 48th Street on October 16, 1952, and starred John Kerr who went on to fame as the leading man in the musical *South Pacific*.

The play was well received. *The New York Daily News* called *Bernardine* one of Broadway's major successes, "a little sweetheart of a comedy."[19]

Said the *New York Times*, "the author knows more about young people than anyone writing for the stage today."[20]

Brooks Atkinson called the play "wonderfully artless and fresh."[21]

Bernardine ran on Broadway for a respectable 152 performances. Chase thought part of the difficulty in presenting the play was that it was produced in a proscenium style rather than in the arena style that she had originally envisioned. When the play was produced in Denver two years later at the University of

Denver Theatre, the director Edward Levy staged the play in the arena style, and this was the staging that was published by the Dramatists' Play Service.

Bernardine went on to movie fame starring Pat Boone, a relatively unknown singer who became a household name.

The debut of the film of *Bernardine* took place in Denver in 1957. Both Pat Boone and his wife attended.

Twentieth Century Fox produced the film. Chase helped adapt her play for the screen with veteran screenwriter Theodore Reeves, but this time she did not actively participate in the filming.

The movie introduced the public to Pat Boone, a young singer who was selected on the chance that he might be able to give Elvis Presley, who was under contract at a rival studio, some competition. Several songs were added including "Love Letters in the Sand," sung by Boone. The song became a hit that topped the music charts for many months. The film also starred the venerable movie star Janet Gaynor in her last Hollywood role. Richard Sargent was cast as one of Beau's friends. He later went on to star in the popular television series *Bewitched*.

Critics felt that the play was much better and that the movie was not as sensitive and humorous.

A NEW LIFE

Chase now lived a comparatively quiet life. She said the Broadway crowd didn't know her and that if she needed to be in New York, she only stayed at the Algonquin just long enough for rewrites during rehearsals and to do some shopping at her favorite boutiques.

"As soon as a play is launched," she told an interviewer, "I immediately get on a plane and fly home to my family in Denver."[22]

Many struggles and challenges occurred before Chase's boys found their niches and settled down.

Of all the boys, Colin was the most intellectual. In his letters written while attending school in the late 1950s, he comments on Castro's politics and his enjoyment of *No Time for Sergeants*, a popular television series. He reads the classics and enjoys discussing his mother's work. He probes *Middlemarch* and Willa Cather's *My Antonia*, and he gives his opinions on the Eisenhower-Stevenson presidential campaign. Youngest son Jerry is less of a letter writer than his brothers. There is a breezy dialogue that consistently runs throughout the letters of both Colin and Michael. They seem to be comfortable exchanging thoughts, ideas, and concerns about their own lives. Both parents are never short of giving advice. When Michael has his marriage difficulties, they respond with support for him and assure him that he will find the right partner.

Bob and Mary Chase's marriage continued to have some rocky moments as well. This was not a surprise considering all the separations that they had from one another and from Mary's frequent mood swings. Despite their ups and downs, they remained together.

Each son's career path took some detours along the way, and so did their personal lives. Michael married in the early 1950s and lived with his first wife in Virginia and became the father of two daughters, the Chases' first grandchildren. After he and his first wife divorced, Michael moved to New York and married Irene Kane, a former model and actress, a celebrity herself, who took on the name of Chris Chase and wrote a best-selling book, *How to Be a Movie Star or A Terrible Beauty Is Born.*

When Mary received a copy of the *Dallas Times Herald* review of Chris's book, she proudly stored it in an envelope and wrote on the outside, "Ain't that a riot!"[23]

After many attempts at a career in the theater, Michael became the director of the State University of New York's public television station in Albany. Colin married in the late 1950s and together he and his wife, Joyce, had five children. Colin became a Jesuit priest, earned a PhD at Harvard, and then began an academic career in medieval studies at the University of Toronto. Jerry met his wife, Mary, at the University of Colorado. They moved to New York where Jerry acted in plays. Soon after they became the parents of four little ones. He then became an academic advisor and a playwright. His play *Cinderella Wore Combat Boots* (1980) is still in publication and remains a popular choice by high schools.

Eventually Bob and Mary Chase were the grandparents of eleven children.

Though the family was often separated from one another, they all kept in close touch and looked forward to family reunions whenever they could make them work.

19

TELEVISION

After *Mrs. McThing* and *Bernardine* appeared on Mary Chase Alley in 1952, the theater climate that had permitted Chase's comic fantasies to entertain took a turn. The times were more positive and optimistic, and there was less need for escape. Thought-provoking plays by Ionesco, Pinter, and Beckett appeared as did bedroom comedies by playwrights like Neil Simon and Jean Kerr who focused on the comfortable post–World War II lifestyle that masses of Americans were experiencing. Instead of a chicken in every pot, there was a Chevrolet in every suburban driveway.

Another reason for this change was the American public's enchantment with the new entertainment medium of television. It began in the late 1940s; by the early 1950s, half of the American public owned television sets. The Golden Age of Television had begun.

At first the medium did not attract the talent needed to draw an audience. The true entertainment professionals were still working on Broadway or in Hollywood or on radio and still skeptical of this new technical innovation. Milton Berle, a lesser-known comedian, took the chance and became an instant hit. So popular was his reception that he came to be known as Mr. Television. His *Texaco Star Theatre* ran from 1948 to 1953, and his success helped to draw other talented professionals into the ring. It was not long before television was producing very popular variety shows attracting entertainers like Sid Caesar, Imogene Coca, and Jackie Gleason.

Along with variety shows, comedies and dramas made a strong entry into the market. Sports and news broadcasts followed.

Families gathered around their sets to watch shows that featured a wide range of news, sports, and entertainment. There were crime shows, mystery and science fiction shows, and wrestling matches, but only four networks provided the airwaves from which viewers could choose their fare. The television stations were highly competitive.

All four of the broadcasting companies produced what was known as anthology dramas. Live television drama was, in essence, the legitimate theater's contribution to the new medium; such shows were regarded as prestige events and were afforded respect accordingly.

Dramatic adaptations by masters like Shakespeare, Charlotte Brontë, and George Bernard Shaw were offered, as were original dramas by more recent playwrights. Paddy Chayefsky's *Marty* was extremely popular as was *Requiem for a Heavyweight* by Rod Serling, best known for his series, *The Twilight Zone*. Among the shows producing anthology dramas were *The Goodyear TV Playhouse*, *Kraft Television Theatre*, *Studio One*, *US Steel Hour*, *Playhouse 90*, *Omnibus*, *DuPont Show of the Month*, and *Hallmark Hall of Fame*.

Though Mary Chase herself, as a playwright, was not widely recognized, the plays and sketches she wrote were becoming very familiar to the public. That is not to say that the press did not notice her success. Many reporters asked for interviews during this time, and many articles were written about her for national publications. "My Life with Harvey" appeared in *McCalls*, an interview with Chase was published in *Cosmopolitan*, and a several page photo spread on *Mrs. McThing* was featured in *Life Magazine* and began with a photo of Helen Hayes and Brandon deWilde on the front cover.

Chase's first entry into television came during the time *Mrs. McThing* was appearing on Broadway. A scene from the show was performed on the popular *Ed Sullivan Show* (1948 to 1971).

OMNIBUS

The year after *Bernardine* debuted, Chase and Helen Hayes continued their association when Chase wrote two sketches, *Irish Linen* and *Mom and Leo*, for the CBS television show *Omnibus* and that starred Helen Hayes.

The Ford Foundation had created the program *Omnibus* to appeal to the more educated sector of the population. It ran on Sundays at 4:00 p.m. Eastern Standard Time on CBS from 1952 to 1961 and was hosted by Alistair Cooke, who, at the beginning, was an unknown Englishman. *Omnibus* presented diverse programming on science, the arts, and the humanities and introduced a variety of fare. Viewers watched new plays, classical music concerts, and comedy sketches. Among other important contributors besides Mary Chase were Leonard Bernstein, William Saroyan, and Jonathan Winters.

The first Chase sketch, *Irish Linen*, was a story of a little old proprietress in a Dublin linen shop who is confronted by a rushed American tourist.

The second sketch, *Mom and Leo*, was a dramatization about a mother (Helen Hayes) who attempts to convince her son Leo (Robert Strauss) that a steady job would be the best thing for him, and after some zany theatrics, ends by convincing herself otherwise.

Another Chase entry was a thirty-minute adaptation of *Mrs. McThing* starring Helen Hayes and Bea Arthur (later star of the Broadway hit *Mame*). It was aired on *Omnibus* on March 9, 1958.

In 1972 *Omnibus* broadcast the second televised version of *Harvey* (see *Dupont Showcase* discussion for first telecast). It was presented on Sunday, March 22, 1972, on CBS at 9:00 p.m. Eastern Standard Time and starred Jimmy Stewart and Helen Hayes who re-created the roles of Elwood and Veta that they had recently performed in a successful revival of *Harvey* on Broadway in 1970. Jesse White again re-created his role as Wilson. The program also featured Arlene Francis as Mrs. Chumley, Madeline Kahn as Nurse Kelly, and Fred Gwynne as the cab driver.

DUPONT SHOW OF THE MONTH

The DuPont Showcase, a monthly ninety-minute television series that ran on CBS from 1957 to 1961, presented the first of three television performances of *Harvey* in September 1958. Comedian Art Carney starred in the role of Elwood. The supporting cast included Charlotte Rae as Veta, Fred Gwynne as Wilson, Larry Blyden as Dr. Sanderson, and Elizabeth Montgomery (who later starred in the popular television series *Bewitched*) as Nurse Kelly.

HALLMARK HALL OF FAME

The *Hallmark Hall of Fame* began in 1951. Early programs included classical works of Shakespeare, biographies on outstanding individuals like Florence Nightingale, and popular Broadway plays such as *Harvey*, *Dial M for Murder*, and *Kiss Me Kate*.

As recently as 1996 *Harvey* was brought again for the third time to the small screen with Harry Anderson, Swoosie Kurtz, and Leslie Nielsen starring in a made for television filmed version and again presented by *The Hallmark Hall of Fame* on CBS.

THE 1990 VIDEO INTRODUCED BY JIMMY STEWART

In 1990, Universal Studios introduced a VHS version of *Harvey*. To help attract buyers, Jimmy Stewart recorded an introduction to the film. Stewart spoke of his affinity for Harvey, calling him "a very close friend of mine." He praised Chase's writing, Henry Koster's directing, and Josephine Hull's Oscar-winning acting, and he mentioned how Hull had the most difficult challenge because she had to be "in between." She couldn't believe in Harvey, yet she couldn't help herself for sometimes believing in Harvey. He recalled a favorite incident of his when he was re-creating his role of Elwood P. Dowd in the London revival of *Harvey*. He chuckled that once at a matinee a child stood up during act 2 and yelled from the audience, "Where's the rabbit?" He also recalled meeting up with a poorly dressed gentleman who followed him down the street once and asked him if Harvey was with him. He told him that Harvey had a cold and had decided to stay home. "Well," replied the gentleman, "give him my regards." At the end of the introduction he suggested that while watching *Harvey* the audience could feel that they "had a friend," and that he hoped the video would bring *Harvey* into one's home anytime they wanted to see him.[1]

The VHS was an instant bestseller and helped Universal Studios reach its financial goals. The DVD of *Harvey* continues to be in demand, and movie channels still periodically schedule viewings.

Mary Chase could certainly feel good about her representation in the new medium of television and of being in good company with other outstanding luminaries of the time such as William Saroyan, Thornton Wilder, and classical playwrights like William Shakespeare.

2O

LADIES FIRST

Mary Chase Alley went back to being Shubert Alley, and Chase reacquainted herself with her typewriter and began to pursue new interests. No longer did she use the paper box stage and thread spools to fashion her plays. She told an interviewer that every time she looked at them she developed a case of "night tremors."[1]

THE MANY LIVES OF LORETTA

After the successes of *Mrs. McThing* and *Bernardine*, Chase's next project took on several different manifestations based on the same plot. First it was a play called *Lolita*, but the name quickly changed to *Loretta* due to the coincidental debut of *Lolita*, a new book by Vladimir Nabokov. Then it became a book called *Loretta Mason Potts*. Then the play was restaged and renamed *Mickey*. Chase at one point even tried to make *Loretta* into a musical.

From the moment the reader is introduced to the story of Loretta Mason Potts, it is hard not to be drawn into the art of the author's imaginative ways:

> Colin Mason was ten years old before he learned he had an older sister. And he never forgot this day—because things were never the same again. It was on a Saturday morning in late September he found out about her. But there was nothing to tell him that morning when he woke up in his little bedroom under the gables of the big house that this day would be very different from all the other Saturdays he had known. The woodbine outside, turning crimson in the autumn sun—why didn't it begin to shake and jiggle and whisper to him? "Oh-Oh Colin—you just wait! Today is the day, Colin"—or else "We know something you don't know!"[2]

There are three resident children in the Mason household when Colin Mason, the oldest, overhears in the grocery store that another Mason named Loretta disappeared seven years ago. He learns that his mother and Loretta went to the farm of Mr. and Mrs. Potts to buy some milk and that while her mother was making her purchase, Loretta wandered off to a nearby hill and discovered a magical miniature castle where a countess, a general, and Sir Edward lived. Loretta too became tiny and was embraced with unconditional love from the castle's residents. After Colin hears the story, the three children seek out the hill and figure out how to diminish themselves and enter the castle and are then also doted upon by Loretta's friends. Their mother soon follows them and shrinks herself as well. Loretta is upset that her family has barged into her little world and runs away. The countess ties up the mother and children who have learned the secret and when Loretta discovers this, she enlarges herself and figures out how to rescue them. In the end she realizes the importance of her family.

Because Chase's children and their friends were off to new adventures, she convinced the four children of her friend Margaret Perry Fanning, daughter of Antoinette Perry, to come every Monday and listen to the latest chapter. The story was completed in 1953.

The first version, the play *Loretta*, was performed in 1954 at the Barter Theatre in Abingdon, Virginia, where Mary's son Michael was a part of the company and where *Mrs. McThing* had originally tried out. Six Broadway producers came to see the play with the possibility of bringing it to New York. It was suggested by one of the producers that Chase rewrite the play around a minor character in the play that would star Tallulah Bankhead, then a popular Broadway actress. Chase agreed to work on this.

While she was starting to write a new version of the play for Bankhead, *Loretta* became the book, *Loretta Mason Potts*, which was originally published in 1958 by Lippincott and illustrated by Harold Berson. The friendly black-and-white simple line drawings bring the words to life. Chase dedicated the book to Karl, Toni, Tag, and Claire Fanning—"the charming children for whom she wrote this story several years ago."[3] The book was a runner-up for the prestigious Dorothy Canfield Fisher children's book award in 1959. It has consistently been published since then and is considered a classic that still entices new readers. In 2014 the publication rights were turned over to the *New York Review of Books* Children's Collection. Since its original publication in 1958, it has never been out of print.

One of Mary's earliest admirers wrote Mary Chase a letter after the book was published:

Dear Mrs. Chase,

I read your book, *Loretta Mason Potts* and enjoyed it. I would appreciate it if you would write me a letter and include a picture of yourself and a list of your other books. Thanks, A faithful reader, Cindy Jones (Des Moines, Iowa)[4]

By 1960, Chase was hard at work putting the final touches on the vehicle for Tallulah Bankhead that she titled *Midgie Purvis*. During this time the National Children's Theatre Conference of the American Educational Theatre Association (AETA) held its annual meeting in Denver and honored Chase with the Monte Meacham Award for "contributing greatly to theater arts for children." A production of *Loretta* was presented to the members of AETA at the Bonfils Theatre in Denver. She dedicated the play to the AETA for encouraging her with her work.

Eight years later Chase revised *Loretta* once more and renamed it *Mickey*. Mickey, a male, replaced the original female character of Loretta. Chase added many innovative staging effects including puppets that played the part of the castle fairies and mingled with the life-size figures of the Mason and Potts families. The play was published by the Dramatists Play Service in 1969 and made its debut at Denver's experimental Changing Scene Theatre in December of 1968.

MIDGIE PURVIS AND TALLULAH

Midgie Purvis opened at the Martin Beck Theatre in New York City on February 1, 1961. It was directed by actor Burgess Meredith after another actor, Jose Ferrer, resigned. It had only twenty-one performances but its star, Tallulah Bankhead, received a coveted Tony Award nomination as best actress.

One review that was written by *New York Times* critic John Chapman observed:

> Putting playwright Mary Chase and Tallulah together is an inspiration, like inventing the martini. Mrs. Chase is daffy and sweet and Miss Bankhead is realistic and tart. Miss Bankhead's performance is a joy to behold and hear, for it bubbles with the comic spirit and falls in perfectly with the playwright's nutty notions. Since Mrs. Chase thinks that children are more interesting and smarter than most people, the bulk of the comedy is about Miss Bankhead's mad adventures with them.[5]

Chapman felt the play was not just a slight comic invention; "Like other Chase plays," such as *Harvey* and *Mrs. McThing*, "it carries a gentle warning to the human race that they should act more human."[6]

Midgie Purvis was based on a lot of thinking Chase had done for several years about the problem of middle-aged women whose children have left home and whose husbands are busy men.[7]

In the play Midgie Purvis is a well-to-do matron whose son pleads with her to make a respectable appearance in front of his future in-laws. Instead Midgie leaves her mansion, dons a wig to look like Whistler's Mother, and becomes a babysitter for three children. She hides herself from her friends by taking an apartment behind the Wee Wee Sweete Shop. She even prints ads to try and lure others into what she calls the Mother Machree Club:

> You dear girls in the middle years. Give up the fight for youth. Come out from under the dryer; you've nothing to lose but the girdle. Skip the unhappy adjustments of middle age. Leap like a deer into old age. Join the Mother Machree Club and love life again. You too can have the best seat on the bus. You too can wander the world passing out the fond embraces of sweet old age to fine young men.[8]

Eventually Midgie's babysitting services are no longer needed and Midgie is forced to come back to reality. By this time her son has realized his mistake and has ended his engagement to his uppity fiancé.

The reviews were mixed. Critics cited the clever staging, especially Bankhead's use of a long telephone cord that tangled her into funny positions and the rapid fire pace that occurred during the many transitions of Bankhead from one character to another.

Nonetheless, the play did not survive. Among the reasons offered was the fact that there was a snowstorm on opening night and that a newspaper strike was taking place that prevented reviews from being quickly distributed.

A disappointed Chase returned home and vowed once again to stay away from Broadway.

MORE WORK

In between writing *Loretta Mason Potts* and *Midgie Purvis*, Chase made several other contributions to the theatrical world. *The Prize Play*, a one-act play about a sixth-grade girl who pushes her way into directing a theater production with showy women, chase scenes, and keystone cops, was presented at the University of Denver Theatre in 1959; *The Dog Sitters*, about a woman who pampers her dogs and hires two young mischievous girls to babysit for her poodles while she goes on a cruise, was produced in Phoenix, Arizona, at the Phoenix Playhouse in 1966. Another completed play, *Punish Willie*, about a homeless man who saves a young girl before he leaves the earth, was written in 1967. Of a more serious subject than her light-hearted comedies, the play was neither published nor produced.

WICKED WICKED LADIES

Ten years after Chase published her first book in 1958, a second published book also won a nomination for the Dorothy Canfield Fisher Award. It too had many variations. First it was called *The Wicked Wicked Ladies in the Garden*. It then became *The Wicked Wicked Ladies in the Haunted House*. Again, for a time it was rewritten to be a play. The first version was illustrated by Don Bolognese and was originally published by Knopf in 1968. Scholastic Services, a firm that caters to publishing important children's books, took over the publishing in 1971. The drawings are intricate colorful etchings of mansions and pigeons and the seven elegant sisters. Knopf published a newer edition retitled *The Wicked Wicked Pigeon Ladies in the Haunted House* in 2003. The illustrations of Peter Sis are more abstract and subtle. Today the original editions are collectors' items.

The story goes that Maureen Swanson is known among the other children in her neighborhood as a "hard slapper, a shouter, a loud laugher, a liar, a trickster and a stay after-schooler."[9]

One day she disobeys her parents by breaking into the grounds of the old Messerman place where there are seven portraits of the elegant sisters. She steals a pigeon bracelet belonging to the sister Ingrid. The enchanted sisters are determined to make Maureen give back the bracelet. They transport her back to the previous century when the house was new and the seven sisters were spoiled and living with their loving parents. The Messermans let Maureen stay because they think she's lost. The sisters hound Maureen for the bracelet. She finally surrenders it and the seven girls transform themselves into pigeons and fly away. Their distraught parents pine away and die of loneliness. Maureen leaves the house, returns to the present, and goes home, now understanding how her naughty behavior hurts her family.

Details in the tale from the past era to which Maureen returns introduce the reader to another time in history and point out a way of life when the means of staying warm were stoves and fireplaces, and hot water bottles placed in their beds at night. Chase also has the daughters make charity visits to poor families just like the ones she made with her mother when she was growing up.

For several years after *Wicked Wicked Ladies* was published, Chase worked on a play production of the book. At this point in her life, she liked to give Denver the first opportunity to produce her plays. During this time, the Bonfils Theatre was in transition and had become primarily a children's theater with longtime Bonfils producer Henry Lowenstein still remaining at the helm. After Helen Bonfils passed away in 1972, her attorney, Donald Seawell, a New York transplant, became the executor of the Bonfils Foundation. Soon after Miss Helen's death, he began to make plans to build a new and more expansive theater complex that would include the Bonfils Theatre Company. He purchased the land where the Curtis Street Theater District had stood, razed the vintage theaters, and in its place erected the vast Denver Center for the Performing Arts Complex. The opening of the venue took place in 1986.

In the meantime Lowenstein ran the children's theater for a while, and then purchased the theater from Donald Seawell. Six months later, the doors of the theater closed and Lowenstein moved to a different venue on Santa Fe Drive.

In the midst of the turmoil, Lowenstein and Chase had difficulty trying to get *Wicked Wicked Ladies* produced. Correspondence between executor Donald Seawell, Mary Chase, and Henry Lowenstein indicates that all kinds of miscommunications and infighting occurred.[10] Actors' Equity was unable to approve of permission for the actors chosen to perform the play. After months of trying to work through the details, the project was finally scrapped.

As was true for all of Chase's efforts to produce her plays, in the final analysis, the producers, the directors, the playwright, and the playwright's agent all factored into a final outcome. In Chase's career, the degrees of success varied starting with the Federal Theatre Project, moving on to the Perry-Pemberton "skylarks," to three more Broadway productions, and several regional productions. Sometimes her choices were made because of the opportunities given to her at the moment. That was true of deciding to write *The Next Half Hour* the year after *Harvey*. Sometimes the choices were financial. Her decision to sell *Sorority House* to RKO rather than take a chance on another Broadway production was determined because she needed money immediately. Sometimes they had to do with personal choices such as deciding to produce *Mrs. McThing* at the Barter Theatre in Abingdon, Virginia, where her son was a member of the production company or when she hired a fellow Irishman to produce the musical of *Harvey* instead of accepting offers made by composers Rogers and Hammerstein and Leonard Bernstein.

In the long run, Mary Chase's choices were as unique as her writings. She listened to her own heart and accepted the consequences.

2 |

PROFESSOR MARY

In the spring of 1964, Mary Chase entered a classroom at the University of Denver to teach a course on playwriting. The theater had been good to her, and she wanted to give back by helping to encourage potential talent.

She told an interviewer that one of the reasons she taught her course was that she believed the university could be a great incubator for playwriting and that community theater could then be a positive springboard for a beginning playwright. Before she had moved onto Broadway, she had begun her own career at the local level with the Denver Federal Theatre Project and then with the University of Denver Civic Theatre.

With the sunlight pouring in through the windows and a view of the greening concourse outside her classroom, Chase addressed her students. She began by telling them that she was there to teach craftsmanship but that learning how to write a play would only take them so far. "After that," she said, "you just have to run with it. My plays have been most successful when I've followed my hunches."[1]

In her lectures she did not share the incidents in her personal life that had influenced her: the whimsical ways of her Irish uncles, her belief in the supernatural, her reporting days covering society and local politics, or her bouts with authority. She left the discovery of her students' life inspirations to be explored individually.

HOW TO BEGIN

"A play," she explained, "begins with an idea, one's 'raw material' that the playwright can easily keep twisting."[2]

She also told them that it was better in the beginning to start with an incident that struck them than to begin with a message they wanted to get across. Calling the two opposing ideas subjective and objective, she pointed out that *Harvey* started with the incident of a dream about a psychiatrist chasing a rabbit that was subjective and that if she had begun with the objective, she would have had in mind writing a play where the message of humanity, love, and imagination were the ultimate goal.

The importance of taking the audience into consideration was of paramount importance, she said. "At first your audience is 'your enemy to overcome.' You must meet your audience at the point where they are at this moment in time and interest them, hold them, and try to lift them."[3]

There are many comments throughout *Harvey* and all her plays that address subjects of interest to the public that apply to the moment but that also stand the test of time. In *Harvey*, many offhanded observations are made about women, mental health, and society in particular. The psychiatrist, Dr. Sanderson, has a "hard shell." Veta dresses down her daughter for acting too smart. Mrs. Chumley is anxious to see the house of the hosts of the party that she and Dr. Chumley are going to be attending.

Chase also spoke about the subject of genre and explained what she thought to be the difference between writing comedy and tragedy. She said that comedy became tragedy when the character and the situation were no longer funny. Chase tried both types and acknowledged that her comedies were more successful than her dramas. We can laugh at Elwood's naiveté rather than feel he's somewhat delusional, and we can enjoy the repartee of Dr. Sanderson and his lovesick nurse rather than find them hopeless.

THE CRAFT OF WRITING

After she had generalized about playwriting, she turned her class's attention to the basics.

The most important aspect of a play is the creation of its structure. "Drama is the art of crisis; you glue scenes together with suspense."[4] She highly recommended studying melodramas because they were so good at showing suspense. How is the woman tied to the railroad tracks going to be rescued? What happens to the heroine when she can't pay the rent? Will Elwood P. Dowd get to keep his friend, *Harvey*?

"A play is like a building—one false line and the structure collapses."[5]

Chase felt that characters were "adaptable." Often her characters changed sexes, ages, or characteristics. She said that her characters were like algebra. The symbols could be transferred from one to another. At one point when Chase was writing *Mrs. McThing*, the witch was a male warlock rather than a woman. Harvey began as a canary, then became a woman before he wound up as a giant white rabbit.

"Essence follows form," she declared. "Once the plot is established the characters can then move the scenes with their actions and their dialogue."[6]

Chase wanted her major characters to be developed in more depth than her minor ones. Principal characters needed to be "given full dimension and singular natures."[7] She felt that Elwood Dowd was more than an "amiable dipsomaniac" because he is warm and human. He hands out his card to everyone he meets and he wants to do whatever makes his sister happy. He dresses in classical tweed, and he invites everyone to his house for dinner.

Chase explained that her minor characters could be stereotypes such as gossipy social climbers like Mrs. Chauvenet and Dr. Chumley's wife in *Harvey*, devoted servants in *Mrs. McThing*, and doting parents in *The Dog Sitters*.

For Chase it was natural to base most of her characters on real people. Again she avoided getting too personal. Though there are many biographical incidents that may have subtly influenced her scenes and characters in *Harvey*, only in the case of Elwood Dowd did she mention that the character was based on people she knew. There is no acknowledgment that Dr. Chumley bears a resemblance to an innovative psychiatrist doing work near her home in Denver or of male reporters at the *Rocky Mountain News* who behaved like the misogynistic character of Dr. Sanderson.

Chase also doesn't go into detail about how giving her characters silly names, descriptions, or actions can make them come to life. In *Mrs. McThing*, the characters of Stinker and Poison Eddie Shellenbach reinforce the traits of the gangsters, and in *Bernardine* Wormy Weldy connotes a rather odious human being. Stinker was a common word in the Chase household. Son Jerry once wrote a postcard to a friend of his when he was traveling with his family on a cruise ship going to London. Said Jerry to his friend Tom, "I hope you're not riding your bike with Bobby, that stinker."[8]

From Chase's *Me Third* failure, she had learned that besides laughter and love, a character must have beauty. She stressed that in order for there to be beauty in a play, there must be a "heart-line, a warmth that speaks to the emotions of an entire theater audience."[9] In other words, *Harvey* is not just about the antics of an invisible rabbit. The "heart-line" is about realizing that though Elwood is an eccentric, he is still loveable.

Chase then addressed the importance of capturing the eye and the ear of the audience in ways that go beyond taking the plot, the characters, and the theme further along. Some of this is the business that the director or the actor is responsible for, but Chase's stage directions also move the characters. For example, she has Elwood clear a space for Harvey to sit in Dr. Chumley's office, and she makes the play move quickly because of her entrance and exit instructions. The audience listens to the fast-moving dialogue stated by the characters in *Harvey*. Veta calls Wilson a "white slaver," because the attendant is dressed in white and is trying to lock her up and describes Dr. Sanderson, the psychiatrist, as a "liar" with "close-set eyes." Dr. Sanderson thinks Elwood is corny and as "outdated as a cast-iron deer."

Chase shared with her students that originally she tried to imagine the visual with a paper box set and the use of thread spools for characters that she moved around. She also encouraged her students to read to friends and acquaintances to see if their plays could hold the interest of an audience.

GETTING TO PRODUCTION

Chase believed that the goal of every playwright was to see their play brought to life on a stage with real actors. Unless a play was produced for an audience, it hadn't reached completion.

It was difficult, she said, to be such a long way from New York when she began her career. She suggested to her students that they use their local surroundings in which their stories could take place. "The stories performed in the community of the original occurrence would make past events come alive for the present audience. A student can use the lumber of an old plot to build a new play."[10] With the exception of *Julius Caesar*, she did not explore or make comparisons to current award-winning plays or to classic plays that her students could read in order to further understand the importance of a play's structure.

Other than suggesting that her students try to begin with local productions, she skirted other means they might take in order to get their plays produced. She did not share her fierce determination to achieve. No mention was made of her own quest to meet Andy Slane, the initiative she took to contact Antoinette Perry, or the decision she made to hire an agent to help persuade the Federal Theatre Project executives to produce *Me Third*.

She did spend quite a bit of time on drama critics' roles in the success of a play and stressed that the bottom line on whether a play was successful was word of mouth and the cost of the box office ticket.

"Critics are primarily newspapermen making a living by criticizing the theater. They come forth with an opinion," the former newspaperwoman said. "It's their job." She went on: "Critics should be considered reviewers rather than critics. They are reporting what they see on a particular night. They are more influenced by the audience."[11] Chase was known to contradict herself at different moments in her life. Her observation on critics diminishes the importance that critics played during her first production of *Now You've Done It* when the audience laughed and the critics panned the work and essentially were responsible for the play's short run.

She cautioned her students to avoid thinking of the critics and to think instead about the audience for whom they were writing.

For Chase, critics' reviews did not make her a better playwright. In her mind they were not able to figure out why *Harvey* was a success and could only look at the surface of the plot rather than finding any deeper meaning. "They saw it as a play about an amiable drunk. It wasn't a play about an amiable drunk at all. It would never have pleased as many people as it has if it had been a play like that."[12]

For Chase's final assignment she asked her students to write a play based on a tragedy that had occurred locally in Colorado, the 1864 massacre of Indians at Sand Creek. The students were to use Shakespeare's tragedy *Julius Caesar* for the basis of the structure of their plays.

Chase was well received by her students. They were impressed with her stature and her devotion to reading their work and encouraging them to do better.

22

AGELESS *HARVEY*

It was not enough for *Harvey* to have experienced a record-breaking Broadway run. After four and a half years and three touring companies, the demand for productions of *Harvey* kept right on going.

Chase once said that she was told "not a day goes by when *Harvey* is not playing in a theater in some place around the world." She added, "Thank God."[1]

Along with three television productions, there were two major revivals in New York and London.

BROADWAY AGAIN

The first revival of *Harvey* took place on Broadway in 1970 twenty years after the release of the film starring Jimmy Stewart. Stewart re-created his "favorite" film and stage role, and Helen Hayes played his sister, Veta Louise. Stephen Porter directed the play that took place at the ANTA Playhouse. The production was scheduled for a limited performance of five weeks but was extended for five weeks because it was so well received. James Stewart won a Drama Desk Award for his role as Dowd, and Helen Hayes was nominated for a Tony Award for her role as Veta Louise Simmons. A year later the pair repeated their performances in the 1972 televised production of *Harvey* on the CBS *Hallmark Hall of Fame*.

LONDON AGAIN

Once again *Harvey* played London in 1975 and once again Jimmy Stewart re-created his role as Elwood for the last time. There were more rave reviews and the play's run lasted six months.

MR. STEWART GOES TO DENVER

It was on the occasion of the thirty-fifth anniversary of the debut of *Harvey* in 1978 that Chase's *Harvey* played Denver's Bonfils Theatre for a two-week run. The first night was a benefit for the House of Hope, the charity Chase had helped to found and that she had generously supported through the years. Mary and Bob Chase were in attendance. As the curtain fell on the last act, from the back of the auditorium, a tall, slim man stepped forward to congratulate the playwright. Nobody had noticed him sitting in the audience. Jimmy Stewart and his wife, Gloria, had come to pay their respects to Chase. There was a collective whispering from the audience when they recognized the famous actor as he came forward to make a presentation amid a clamoring of applause. Henry Lowenstein, the Bonfils Theater executive director of the production, was speechless.

Reported *Denver Post* society editor Patricia Collins: "Stewart and his wife Gloria flew in from L.A. to honor the playwright, Denver's Mary Chase (Mrs. Robert)."[2] Stewart thanked Chase for introducing him to Harvey, "my lifelong friend." Once again he said that *Harvey* had always been his favorite role. He then presented Chase with a giant sized chocolate bunny and a Steuben crystal rabbit, "reminders of the pleasure *Harvey* had given to millions of theatergoers."[3] After Stewart's speech, Donald Seawell, the theater's representative and the evening's host, read telegrams that were sent from well-wishers including one from Helen Hayes who could not attend the event.

Throughout the years, Denver's theaters would continue to honor their favorite daughter with productions of *Harvey* at Denver's community theaters including a performance in 1963 at Elitch Gardens and at a revival at Central City in 1971 starring Gig Young and Shirley Booth.

HARVEY EVERYWHERE

Harvey continues to regularly make his appearance at theaters throughout the country and the world. It has played at community theaters, high schools, universities, churches, and at almost every American regional theater. In recent years, nationally acclaimed regional theater productions have been staged at Chicago's Steppenwolf Theatre in 1990, at the Shaw Festival in Ontario in 2010, and at Minneapolis's Tyrone Guthrie Theater in 2016.

Between 2017 and 2018, some of the locations where productions of *Harvey* took place included Michigan, Georgia, Virginia, South Dakota, North Carolina, Illinois, New Jersey, Texas, Arizona, and Israel.

Despite the fact that one reviewer of London's *The Guardian* called a 2015 Birmingham, England, production of *Harvey* a "creaky old warhorse,"[4] there is never a dearth of *Harvey* productions from year to year.

No matter how old *Harvey* gets, actors still want their chance to portray the characters and directors want to stage the play on their own terms. In one production a director made the play into the style of a farce. Elwood was dressed in plaid, a harkening back to vaudevillian times and to the zany antics of entertainers like the Marx Brothers. Another director decided to dress the actors in neon bold colors. In the 2017 Court Theatre production in Chicago, a director cast the judge as a woman rather than as the traditional male the original role called for. When another director was asked why he wanted to produce *Harvey* now (in 2017), he said it was because "the glass's half full mentality"[5] is what we need in the country.

*BIG BANG THEORY'*S JIM PARSONS PLAYS ELWOOD

Another *Harvey* revival to gain acclaim occurred in 2012 when Jim Parsons, the Emmy award–winning star of *The Big Bang Theory*, appeared in New York's Roundabout Theatre production at Studio 54. The opening was a star-studded gala, and the production was enthusiastically received.

Jim Parson's performance of Elwood was hailed for its charm and warmth. Parsons complimented the audience because they were "willing to listen" and "to get on board and take the ride." He said there was so much to perform and that the writing was brilliant and still "holds up."[6]

Parson's supporting cast included other actors well known in the entertainment world. Jessica Hecht played Veta Simmons, Carol Kane portrayed Mrs. Chumley, Charles Kimbrough was Dr. Chumley, and *Mad Men*'s Rich Sommer took on the role of Wilson.

Photographs of the set appeared in *Architectural Digest* and gave a director and designer opportunities to create new approaches to staging the classic. For a more inclusive feeling, no curtain separated the audience from the Dowd living room. Turntables were installed to facilitate an easier transition back and forth from the Dowd living room and Chumley's Rest. Five doors were placed strategically so that the entrances and exits could "keep the pace from slowing down."[7]

The audience loved the humor, poignancy, and joy of the play, and members of the cast delighted in recalling their own imaginary friends.

David Rooney of the *Hollywood Reporter* wrote: "The first entry of the 2012–13 Broadway season is an unassuming charmer. Best known for the 1950 film adaptation that starred James Stewart, Mary Chase's Pulitzer-winning 1944 comedy is a delectable mid-century chestnut with an idiosyncratic personality that still sparkles."[8]

Harvey proved once again that he still had something to say.

THE LEGEND LIVES ON

Harvey or his name continues to have guest "appearances" in movies like *Field of Dreams, The Shawshank Redemption, Donnie Darko*, and *Who Framed Roger Rabbit*, and on television shows like *The Tonight Show* and *The Simpsons*.[9]

One of the many humorous references occurred on a segment of the situation comedy *The Gilmore Girls* when Lorelie mentioned the invisible rabbit. "Duck, Harvey," she said when Rory moved the phone cord through Luke's empty diner.[10]

In *Wallace and Gromit: the Curse of the Were Rabbit* (2005), the were-rabbit is a giant rabbit like Harvey and the local vegetable shop is named "Harvey's."

There is a slight similarity between *Harvey* and the cult black comedy *Donnie Darko* (2001). In this film, Jake Gyllenhaal plays a teenager who is plagued by the recurring appearance of a demonic six-foot-tall rabbit named Frank that only he can see and who warns him about the demise of the world in twenty-eight days.

Myriad references to the invisible rabbit who never seems to get old are listed in large numbers on the internet and are updated with regularity.

IS A FILM REVIVAL IN THE FUTURE?

In recent years several Hollywood companies have purchased the rights to re-create a new version of *Harvey*. In 2000 producers Harvey and Bob Weinstein picked up the option with the idea of starring John Travolta in the lead. In 2009 Steven Spielberg bought the rights with the intention of having Tom Hanks play the lead role. Spielberg also considered Robert Downey Jr. and Brad Pitt to play Elwood. As this book is being published, Netflix has picked up the rights and has announced that a new production is in the works.

Harvey, written more than seventy-five years ago, still attracts a massive adoring audience. No doubt there will be many more reincarnations to come.

23

HARVEY, THE MUSICAL

Chase's husband retired in the early 1970s. In 1971, they had purchased a getaway cabin in Elk Falls, a lovely bucolic spot outside of Denver, where the Chases could take long walks with their current dogs, Airedale terrier Max and poodle Las Vegas Jack. Bob spent some of his newly available time fishing in the same ponds where President Dwight Eisenhower had once fished to get away from the public scrutiny that accompanied him when he had visited his wife's parents in Denver while he was in office from 1952 to 1960.

The cabin proved to be a happy gathering spot for family and friends. Albert Brooks, the owner of Denver's Changing Scene Theatre that produced Chase's *Mickey*, once visited Elk Falls and mused: "There was Mary in the mountains cooking for us and wearing pearls."[1]

ENJOYING LIFE

In between their escapes to Elk Falls, Chase continued to pursue her literary life.

The boys were now married with children, and they had all settled down to work in their professions. All three had moved to the east: Colin to Toronto where he was now an associate professor of medieval studies, and Jerry and Michael to New York. Jerry explained why they all moved east. He said it was "the lure of the theater."[2]

The Chases continued to live at their Denver mansion where they regularly entertained their large circle of friends. Clé Cervi Symons, daughter of newspaperman Gene Cevi, recalls going for tea as a young child with her parents and Chase taking her upstairs to see her dollhouse collection. She laughed as she remembered Chase telling her, "You should never put a hat on a bed."[3]

Chase was also gracious to fans and admirers. One day a group of three friends who were starring in *Harvey* at their church paid a spontaneous visit to Chase. They had found her name and address in the Denver phone book and decided to knock on her door and see if they could meet her. She invited them in for tea. They gladly accepted. "She was warm, gracious and lovely," said one of those who attended. After their meeting with Chase, they were inspired by the visit and drove a few blocks to Fairfax between 18th and 19th, where the legend goes Elwood leaned against a lamppost and first met Harvey.[4]

Despite all these diversions, Chase continued to write. In 1974 she published *Cocktails with Mimi*, a comedy about a mother, father, and son who have different ideas on who the son should marry. It had one production at the Barter Theatre. Clifford Ridley of the *National Observer* attended the opening in July of 1973. Though he said the audience laughed from start to finish, he found the play "depressing" and the first act "singularly unfunny." What was most depressing, he declared was the suggestion "that a playwright of demonstrated comic gifts has simply lost her comic ear."[5]

Chase wrote two more plays. *The Tattoo Parlor* about girls calling up and playing pranks much like she used to do was published in 1981. One last effort, a musical version of *Harvey*, remained.

SAY HELLO TO HARVEY

Beginning in 1958 a number of producers started to pursue Chase about turning "her *Harvey*" into a musical. Rogers and Hammerstein of *Oklahoma, Carousel, King and I*, and *South Pacific* fame had tried in vain to get Chase to agree. So had Leonard Bernstein and Danny Kaye.[6] It took twenty more years before a musical of *Harvey* became a reality.

Initially Chase refused because she didn't think that either a musical or a television series of *Harvey* "would be suitable."[7]

The holdout only lasted until 1978 when Michael McAloney, a young Irish American producer, called Chase on the phone in Denver. "Young man," she skeptically replied, "I presume you want to talk about doing a musical version of *Harvey*. You're wasting your time." She did invite him to dinner though. She asked him what he thought was the meaning of *Harvey*. Said McAloney, "If you possess a basic goodness, if you're good at heart, you're allowed to see certain things that other people can't." She consented to do the musical with one catch; he needed to agree that she could stop him if she didn't like it.[8]

McAloney got Toronto producers Ed and David Mirvish to finance the tryout in Toronto at the Royal Alexandra Theatre.

The production cast and crew had impeccable credentials. Leslie Bricusse signed on to write the music for Chase's script. He had composed scores for the Broadway hits *Stop the World I Want to Get Off* and *Roar of the Greasepaint-The*

Smell of the Crowd and his songs "What Kind of Fool Am I" and "The Candy Man" had topped the music charts. Donald O'Connor (of *Singing in the Rain* fame, which had debuted in 1952) took on the role of Elwood. A cast of thirty, twelve of them Canadians, supported him. Tony Award–winner Mel Shapiro was selected to be the director. Chase's son Michael served as the stage manager. There were nineteen musical numbers with titles like "Smalltown, U.S.A.," "The Wednesday Forum," "I Recommend Pleasant," and "Say Hello to Harvey."[9]

In 1981 *New York Magazine* dedicated its fall issue to upcoming events in the arts and listed *Say Hello to Harvey* as en route to Broadway.

The stage was set.

The play debuted to a sellout crowd of 1,497 on September 6, 1981, at Toronto's Royal Alexandra Theatre with Mary Chase in the audience. It received a standing ovation. The reviewers, however, were not as enthusiastic. Though they praised the actors and a few of the songs, there was also a consensus among the three Toronto newspaper reviewers that the musical was too long and that the music mostly got in the way of the story. Chase too was not pleased with the final outcome.

Say Hello to Harvey closed six weeks later on October 17, 1981. The Washington, DC, preview and the Broadway engagement were both canceled.

There have been many postmortems on why *Say Hello Harvey* did not succeed. Leslie Bricusse felt that there were some brilliant moments, particularly the performance of Patricia Routledge who played Veta. He also thought that Donald O'Connor who was in his fifties and ailing did not lend his whole heart to the production.[10]

Many pundits have commented on *Say Hello to Harvey*'s failure. One suggested that works that don't need music should not be produced. In this category along with *Harvey*, he listed musical versions of plays or movies that failed on Broadway: *Gone with the Wind*, *Our Town*, and *Dr. Zhivago*. He did point out that sometimes works are successful and cited *My Fair Lady*, adapted from George Bernard Shaw's *Pygmalion*, as one of the best examples. "*Harvey* was one of those superbly constructed character farces which could only be weakened by adding songs."[11]

Despite the failure of *Say Hello to Harvey*, there continues to be interest in pursuing musical versions of *Harvey*. In October 2017 a Broadway actor, Nic Rouleau, starred in a revue at Feinstein's cabaret in New York where he presented "Broadway Bound 2: The Musicals That Never Came to Broadway." He sings the title song, "Say Hello to Harvey," invites a member of the audience to come up on stage with him, and the "three" of them take a selfie. One can also find a small underground clip of a cast song on YouTube complete with audience applause.[12]

When talking about his lack of success with *Say Hello to Harvey*, Leslie Bricusse said he still had faith that one day *Harvey* would come again to Broadway.

GOING HOME

Let down by her latest effort, Mary Chase returned home to Denver on October 17. Son Michael stayed behind to take care of postproduction details. After all the effort, it was hard for her to put into perspective this setback even after her past phenomenal success.

On October 20, 1981, four days after her return to Denver from the Toronto opening, Chase suffered a heart attack and died. She was seventy-four years old. She had given life her best, and it was time to say "enough."

24

THE CURTAIN FALLS

The family gathered at Crown Hill Cemetery where Chase's body was cremated. Above her buried ashes, a headstone was placed in a spot directly in front of another family plot that largely displayed the name of the HARVEY family. Some say it was one last Mary Chase prank.

A memorial followed at Olinger Mortuary in Denver where those who had known Chase through work and play came to pay their respects to Chase's husband of fifty-three years, their three sons and their wives, and their eleven grandchildren.

A *New York Times* obituary cited Chase's accomplishments:

Mary Chase, the imaginative playwright who became famous and wealthy by creating an invisible rabbit named Harvey that dwelled in the minds of theater and movie audiences all over the world, died Tuesday in Denver, where she was born 74 years ago.[1]

A *Denver Post* editorial read:

Although the play was named for a rabbit, it was a very human play reflecting the warmth and vitality of the human who wrote it. . . . Mary Chase was important in Denver history because of the role she played on a thriving, energetic newspaper—because of her wit—because of her literary skill and important because she was a very nice person.[2]

Condolences poured in from near and far. There were notes from actor Orson Bean, Helen Hayes, and *Mrs. McThing* producer Robert Whitehead. Sympathies were offered too by Chase's local friends including Margaret Perry Fanning, Caroline Bancroft, Al Brooks of the Changing Scene Theatre, and many journalists who had known Bob and Mary Chase since their *Rocky Mountain News* days.

THE FINAL COUNT

Throughout her life, Mary Chase had just kept plodding along. When it was all over, observers could look back and marvel at what she had accomplished.

Mary Chase was the author of fourteen published plays, three screenplays, and two books; the winner of the Pulitzer Prize for Best Drama in 1945 for *Harvey*; the runner-up for best play by the Drama Critics' Circle in 1952 for her play *Mrs. McThing*; and a two-time finalist for the Dorothy Canfield Fisher Award for best children's book for *Loretta Mason Potts* and the *Wicked Pigeon Ladies of the Haunted House.*

Many times both before and after her death, prestigious groups honored her for her contributions. She was the recipient of an honorary doctorate of letters degree from the University of Denver, the William McLeod Reine Award from the Colorado Authors' League, and the Monte Meacham Award from the Children's Theatre Conference of the American Educational Theatre Association. Chase was an honorary lifetime member of The Denver Women's Press Club. Posthumously, she was inducted into the Colorado Women's Hall of Fame and the Colorado Performing Arts Hall of Fame.

Throughout her life she participated in many Denver community activities and supported a wide variety of theatrical organizations. She was a founder of the Denver House of Hope for women alcoholics and an advocate for the Central City Opera Association and the Bonfils Theatre. In 1981 she was appointed an honorary committee member of the American National Theatre Academy.

THE ESSENTIAL MARY

Through the years, friends, associates, and acquaintances offered a variety of opinions about the real Mary Chase.

Wallis Reef, a friend and fellow journalist:
"By all accounts, Mary Chase was high-spirited, athletic, adventurous and fond of practical jokes, which contrasted nicely with her Madonna appearance."[3]

Eleanor Harris, journalist:
"A deeply emotional woman who swung without warning from hilarious gaiety to heavy Irish gloom (and whose) close friends claimed that although most anecdotes concerning Chase were amusing, she seldom smiled and her eyes contained a hint of melancholy."[4]

Gene Cervi, publisher of the *Cervi's Rocky Mountain Journal*:
She had "a mysterious mind."[5]

Lee Casey, longtime friend and fellow journalist:
"Mary always was a woman with a burning hatred of cruelty and injustice. She was anti-fascist by instinct."[6]

Mark Barron, Associated Press:
Mary "never pretended to be anything more than a wife and mother who wrote plays in her spare time."[7]

Michael Chase, eldest son of Mary:
She "detested authority. And she was funny. She worked at what she loved best: at a play in progress. Life [became] vague while the play [became] real."[8]

Margaret Fanning Perry, friend and actress:
"In a way she [was] a gentle bully about her friends' lives. She [managed] you into doing not what you wanted to do, but what [was] right for you to do."[9]

Tom Hilb, son of Mary's friend artist Greta Hilb:
"I loved Mary. She was interesting."[10]

REFLECTIONS FROM MARY

Mary's view of herself was sometimes critical, sometimes philosophical, and many times satirical.

On her success:
"Fifty-fifty—I wanted to be a great playwright and I never made it—I never regretted *Harvey*. I shouldn't have spent so long trying to surpass it."[11]

On her life philosophy:
"I smoke."
    "I have a passion for big hats."
    "I drink. Can you imagine anything more foul than to have written *Harvey* and being a teetotaler?"[12]
    "Look up a little and begin to praise. The world has need of it. In the Bible it says to go in your closet and pray. I'm not ashamed to say I've been in there in my fashion."[13]
    "When you begin to think you're good, you're through."[14]

On religion:
"Studying the history of the Renaissance and the history of the Reformation made me question the church."[15]

On her writing:
"It is only when I am writing that I feel really complete. When I am in one of my writing trances, I am cushioned against the sadnesses and griefs of the world."[16]

On her contemporary playwright peers and how she believed differently:
"These playwrights write plays which succeed or fail. They like to do it, and they make a living. Most of them drive good cars and go to good psychiatrists. When they die, their obituaries are printed in *Variety*. That's how you can always tell if you are a playwright."[17]

On the Denver theatrical community:
"In my fledgling days there was a productive theatrical milieu here in Denver. At present you can't discount the fine work being done by Helen Bonfils and the Civic Theatre—they'll always give a tryout playwright a break if he shows definite promise. They've been wonderful to me when I needed it."[18]

On family:
"And my husband, Bob Chase? In almost every story of this kind, divorce follows success as two follows one. He grew prematurely gray, but he was the Rock of Gibraltar. He suffered but he did not give up."[19]

"I don't believe any career can do justice on your family life. One (life) has to suffer."[20]

On comedians for whom she had great sympathy:
"Twenty-four hours a day the comic is working to make people laugh. And to keep on creating laughter he has to cultivate his own garden of sorrow. It is through sorrow he makes laughter. He must lower his own spirits to the level of desolate human beings in order to sense how to lift them up."[21]

MARY BY THE BOOK

Mary's deeper feelings and emotional ties are often revealed in the lines of her plays and books.

"Doctor—the function of a psychiatrist is to tell the difference between those who are reasonable and those who merely talk and act reasonably."
—Dr. Chumley, *Harvey*

"What terrible force made you hate your mother and prefer the milkman?"[22]
—*Mrs. McThing*

"And when I do go—really go—finally go. . . . I don't want anybody acting like I haven't gone. I don't want anybody saying—we won't act like she's gone. We'll act like she's only stepped into another room. That's the way she'd want it. Well—that's not the way I want it. I want them to scream and yell and howl—for months. I want one of those stars up there to go out—when I go out and never turn on again—I want somebody some place—to miss me."[23]
—*Midgie Purvis*

25

THE FINAL REVIEW

It's difficult to dispute that the endurance of *Harvey* remains Mary Coyle Chase's most outstanding contribution to theater and film. The play and the movie were huge critical and financial successes, and seventy-five years later the play continues to be revived, the movie replayed, and the story discussed. According to author Carolyn Casey Craig, *Harvey* was Chase's "shining hour."[1]

But what about Mary Chase's collective contributions?

UNDER THE RADAR

In 2017 Chris Jones, a *Chicago Tribune* reporter reviewed a new production of *Harvey* that was appearing at the Court Theatre located in Hyde Park near the University of Chicago. In the article he called *Harvey* "one of the most underestimated plays of the 20th century by scholars and historians anyway."[2]

Others have weighed in on the dearth of analysis that has been conducted on the work of Mary Chase. Said one academic, "Mary Chase's comedies, particularly *Harvey*, deserve the serious treatment they have not yet received from critics and even from their more enthusiastic reviewers."[3]

A contemporary film journalist recently commented on "the scant number of scholars who have dissected the film and who have only focused on its engaging fantasy elements and Elwood Dowd's role as an exemplar of gracious humanity and/or non-threatening masculinity."[4]

BY THE LAUGHS

In her own life, Mary Chase was inclined to cover her sorrows with laughter and to make fun of others as a means of self-preservation. It is no wonder that her greatest comedy successes with *Harvey, Mrs. McThing*, and *Bernardine* all trace back to her own experiences.

Harvey in particular is consistently lauded as a great American comedy. The American Film Institute ranks *Harvey* thirty-fifth out of the one hundred best comedy films. Members of the Broadway community were once asked to vote for their choice of the most outstanding comedies and *Harvey* was included along with the stalwarts of *The Man Who Came to Dinner, Arsenic and Old Lace*, and *Life With Father*.[5]

As recently as 2015, a *New York Times* drama critic acknowledged the popularity of *Harvey*: "What's been celebrated lately on Broadway are the dark, biting comedies. . . . Many Broadway plays that ran the longest—*Life With Father, Born Yesterday, Harvey, Barefoot in the Park*—were lighthearted, hopeful comedies."[6]

IN THE WORLD OF FANTASY

Mary Chase lived in a world of spirits and magic, and the characters she created were the mainstays of her fantasies. Loretta Mason Potts resides in a perfect miniature world. Howay runs away from his confining existence in his mansion. Elwood has an imaginary friend.

Chase's works are often compared to other fantasies like *Peter Pan* and *Alice in Wonderland*.

Her beliefs were based on her own enjoyment of entering the world of fantasy. Said the fantasy writer Ursula Le Guin, "Fantasy is true, of course. It isn't factual, but it is true. Children know that. Adults know it too, and that is precisely why many of them are afraid of living."[7]

In an article on "Fantasy in Film," the author Katherine Fowkes links *Harvey* to a number of other fantasy films that occurred in the 1930s and 1940s including *It's a Wonderful Life* (1946), *Topper* (1937), and *Blithe Spirit* (1945), where ghosts or angels are present, and to the iconic children's film *The Wizard of Oz* (1939) where Dorothy enters an imaginary land full of good and evil.

Many contemporary directors enjoy making comparisons among fantasy films and television programs of the 1950s and 1960s like *I Dream of Jeannie, Bewitched*, and *One Flew Over the Cuckoo's Nest* and believe that *Harvey* easily holds its own among newer works of fantasy.

Broadway critics have commented on Chase's treatment of fantasy with different conclusions. The New York drama critic George Jean Nathan believed that Chase was not successful in bringing fantasy to the stage whereas David Sievers, also a New York drama critic, thought Chase helped the audience to create their own fantasies.[8]

In the category of fantasy the American Film Institute lists *Harvey* among its Top 10 along with *Harry Potter*, the recent highly regarded children's fantasy.

AS A FEMALE PLAYWRIGHT

With the exception of *Harvey* in which the protagonist is the unspoken audience, Mary Chase's protagonists are usually women who are either single or widowed. All of her plays and books feature different types of women. Nurse Kelly in *Harvey* is naïve and subservient. Mimi in *Mrs. McThing* is poor but sweet natured and has a strong sense of self. Midgie Purvis is a zany and adventurous middle-aged widow. Unlike some of her fellow Pulitzer Prize female winners, Chase rarely addresses the subject of marriage. Instead her works are more apt to deal with mother-daughter and mother-son relationships or with independent women like Midgie Purvis and *Mrs. McThing*'s Mrs. LaRue.[9]

When writing about female playwrights in the 1980s, Albert Wertheim, an English professor at Indiana University pointed to the strong individual voices of Mary Chase, Lillian Hellman, Clare Boothe Luce, and Lorraine Hansberry who "ushered women playwrights into the mainstream during the years from the Depression to the nineteen fifties despite severe cutbacks in the number of Broadway shows."[10]

He also distinguished Mary Chase from the three other female Pulitzer Prize–winning playwrights who preceded her. "What sets Mary Chase immediately apart is that she does not in her three major plays *Harvey* (1944), *Mrs. McThing* (1952) and *Bernardine* (1952)—deal with the plight of women in society, and she is, moreover, a writer of highly imaginative comedy." In the same book, it is also pointed out that Mary Chase should not be slotted as only a female playwright.[11]

Chase has often been criticized for her portrayal of women. In her article in the *Bright Lights Film Journal*, author Heather Addison writes: "I first watched *Harvey* (1950; director Henry Koster) as an adolescent. Parts of it enchanted me, but I was also alarmed, even shocked, by what I saw. In a memorable sequence, one of the film's main characters, middle-aged Veta Simmons (Josephine Hull), is unexpectedly and unceremoniously abducted, confined, and stripped so that she can undergo hydrotherapy at a mental institution. The image of Veta screaming frantically (and silently) into the small window of a soundproof door after she is taken captive remained with me for years."[12]

George S. Kaufman once asked Chase why there are so few women playwrights. She said it had to do with structure and with women not inclined to like rigid formulas such as algebra and playwriting. Her husband, Bob, said it was because women were too chatty.[13]

THE LITERARY DECREE

Though Mary Chase lamented that she did not achieve the status of a Eugene O'Neill or a Lillian Hellman, the fact that many of her plays appear in anthologies by major critics of the day speaks to the fact that she remains a highly regarded playwright.

Why is it then that she has not attained more recognition for her contributions to the literary world?

"The fact that *Harvey* received the Pulitzer Prize does not mean it appealed to audiences for its literary distinction," declared critic John Toohey. He believed that Tennessee Williams's *Glass Menagerie* portrayed a more truthful reflection of humanity and that the characters and theme as well as the acting all had more depth.[14]

Harvey is sometimes compared to the work of another Pulitzer Prize–winning writer of comedy, William Saroyan, who won for *The Time of Your Life*. Similarities exist between the two protagonists, Elwood P. Dowd in *Harvey* and the genial drunk Joe in *The Time of Your Life*. Critics saw "an edginess, a consciousness of the harsh realities, the struggle of human existence in Joe that they found missing in Elwood."[15]

Albert Wertheim is an ardent proponent of Chase's talent. "The fact that *Harvey* has survived beyond the World War II era, that it is still being successfully performed and enjoyed today, seems proof that the play has more than mere escapism to recommend it."[16] He also acknowledges the literary qualities of two of Chase's other comedies, *Bernardine* and *Mrs. McThing*. Pointing to a deeper meaning in *Bernardine*, he goes on to say, "*Bernardine* is a comedy that has higher sights . . . it suggests that the special world of the kings with its concomitant special ideal visions of womanhood and sexuality, Bernardine Crud of Sneaky Falls, is a necessary part of growing up, a desirable prerequisite for adulthood."[17]

The esteemed critic Walter Kerr weighed in on the significance of *Harvey* on the occasion of the 1970 Broadway revival with Jimmy Stewart when he commented on how the play had held up for a quarter of a century and how its "immense popularity threaten[ed] to obscure its technical brilliance."[18] Pointing out the important themes of *Harvey* as society's perennial need to crush individuals who don't conform and the inability to listen to our fellow humans, another critic wrote: "There is nothing trivial about the themes."[19] Actors in the 2012 Roundabout Theatre production echoed the need especially in modern times for humanity as well as for an optimistic outlook on life wherever way you can find it.[20]

The real controversy remains whether plays that laugh at the foibles of humanity while revealing basic flaws can be as important as works that deal with adversity with often more tragic consequences.

AS AN OUTSIDER

In the tradition of Thornton Wilder's popular play *Our Town* (1939) and the musical *Oklahoma* (1943), Chase's plays and books are almost always placed in the environs around her middle American hometown of Denver, Colorado.

Albert Wertheim believes that not writing about New York or other east coast cities "frees her from social or political issues and casts off the restraints of geography to deftly and sometimes brilliantly use her comic art to present man's eternal conflict between his imaginative world and the constructing world of social forms and social gee-gaw."[21] He goes on to say that a play like *Harvey* shares a common theme with such overtly serious works as Eugene O'Neill's *The Iceman Cometh*, Philip Barry's *Hotel Universe*, and Tennessee Williams's *Glass Menagerie*.

Mary Chase felt it was difficult for writers who did not live in New York to write plays. "Playwriting doesn't seem to be an art that can be mastered anywhere, under any conditions, as in other mediums," Chase once said. "It's a complicated craft that takes a long time to learn and the student needs a certain finish to his apprenticeship that only New York seems able to provide."[22]

Regardless of her belief, she still placed most of her characters in settings that were familiar to her.

THE WRAP

In the countless re-creations of *Harvey*, the discussion continues on about the pros and cons of acknowledging whether Elwood P. Dowd's manner of viewing life is acceptable to society. Regardless of which way the thinking goes, when we see a revival or watch the movie again, we still laugh at the absurdities that the presence of an invisible rabbit can create. That soft smile inevitably shows up on our faces, and we find Elwood totally irresistible.

Equally enduring is Harvey's creator, Mary Coyle Chase, who managed to offer humor, humanity, and fantasy to the public and to live out those themes in her own private life.

Chase scraped her way to success. She was at it from her young contrary days on the playground to her competitive days as a journalist at the *Rocky Mountain News* to her marching days when she supported unions and other minority causes, to her fourteen plays, three screenplays, and two children's stories that "praise and uplift."[23]

In today's society with so many people trying to find answers on how to cope, a story about perseverance, determination, resilience, creativity, and, above all, loyalty is inspiring and uplifting even though the circumstances are very different from the time when Mary Chase met *Harvey*.

EPILOGUE

Rarely do literary contributions consistently remain in the public eye as long as those of Mary Chase's *Harvey*. It's remarkable that the play never stops being produced, the movie continues to be featured at festivals and events, and references to *Harvey* are ongoing. Recognition of *Harvey*'s creator still lags behind this acclaim, and this book is an attempt to bring about more awareness of the extraordinary life and work of Mary Coyle Chase.

All of Chase's published plays, screenplays, and books remain in publication today.

As for the personal aspects of Mary Chase, there are probably many more stories to tell.

Mary and Bob's children each married and had children. At this writing Michael and Jerry are still alive as are ten of the eleven grandchildren born to Michael, Colin, and Jerry and their wives. Colin passed away in 1984 from cancer. Surrounded by his supportive and loving family, Robert Chase passed away in 1990, nine years after his wife.

The eighty-acre property and the cabin and chalet in Elk Falls, Colorado, that were purchased and built by the Chase family in 1971 were sold to the Colorado State Park system in 2006 and are now part of Staunton State Park. As hikers approach the area where the Chase cabin is located, a historic marker reminds them that Mary Chase and her family once occupied the cabin.

The house at 532 West 4th Avenue is now a historic Denver landmark. 505 Circle Drive remains standing and continues to be privately occupied. To this date, no Denver school, library, street, or statue in Denver has been named to honor the achievements of Mary Coyle Chase. The only exception is a plaque recognizing Chase's accomplishments that is housed at the theater in the Denver

Center of the Performing Arts complex. Rarely have any Denver literary figures other than Eugene Field been acknowledged in Denver in a public way. The cabin where Field once lived was moved to a location in Denver's Washington Park where it houses a local branch of the park district. A bronze statue of Field's figures from his "Wynken, Blynken, and Nod" poem stands in front of the cabin. A library also bears his name. Thomas Ferril is remembered for a city lake and his scriptures line the interior walls of the Colorado State Capitol in Denver.

The work and life of Mary Coyle Chase is a uniquely American story that blends the values of those in America who live both east and west. Perhaps this book will mark the beginning of many more tales about *Harvey* and his creator.

NOTES

CHAPTER 1:
THE COYLES AND THE McDONOUGHS

1. Ralph Willingham, "Introduce Them to Harvey: Mary Chase and the Theatre" (master's thesis, East Texas University, 1987), 6.

2. Willingham, "Introduce Them to Harvey."

3. Stephen Leonard and Thomas J. Noel, *Denver: Mining Camp to Metropolis* (Boulder, CO: University of Colorado Press, 1991).

4. Frances Melrose, "Mary Chase: Reporter to Playwright," *Rocky Mountain News* (Denver, CO), February 2, 1977, 8.

5. Sharon R. Catlett, *Farmlands, Forts and Country Life: The Story of Southwest Denver* (Denver: Westcliffe Publishers, 2007), 47–53.

6. Leonard and Noel, *Denver*.

7. Maurice Albert Berger, "Mary Coyle Chase: Her Battlefield of Illusion" (PhD dissertation, University of Denver, 1970), 7.

8. Mary Chase to Alan B. Fisher, undated correspondence, Fisher and Fisher Architectural Records and Correspondence, Denver Public Library.

9. Chase to Fisher.

10. Chase to Fisher.

11. Berger, "Mary Coyle Chase," 12.

12. Wallace Reef, "She Didn't Write It for Money—She Says," *Saturday Evening Post*, September 1, 1945, 109.

13. Reef, "She Didn't Write It for the Money," 51, 109.

CHAPTER 2: LI'L MARY

1. Mary Chase, *The Dog Sitters* (New York: Dramatists Play Service, 1963), 163.

2. Gene Vervalin, *A Walk on the West Side: The Story of an American High School* (Boulder, Colorado: EHV Publications, 1985), 79.

CHAPTER 3: THE LURE OF THE THEATER

1. Shakespeare, William. *The Tragedy of Macbeth.*

2. "Tabor Grand Opera House." http://cinematreasures.org/theaters/19055.

3. "Tabor Grand Opera House."

4. Marsha Sorotick, "Mary Chase: The Woman Behind Harvey," *Irish America*, October/November 2016. https://irishamerica.com/2016/10/mary-Chase-the-woman -behind-harvey/.

5. Sorotick, "Mary Chase."

6. Mary Chase to Karen Wickre, oral transcript, August 1979, Robert L. Chase Papers, 1915–86, Denver Public Library.

7. William Archer, *Playmaking: A Manual of Craftsmanship* (London: Chapman and Hall, 1912) (revised edition, New Haven, CT: Yale University, 2004).

CHAPTER 4: LEAVING THE NEST

1. Clé Cervi Symons interview by Mimi Pockross, Denver, Colorado, November 30, 2017.

2. Chase to Wickre.

3. Chase to Wickre.

4. Chase to Wickre.

5. Chase to Wickre.

6. Chase to Wickre.

7. Donna Born, "The Woman Journalist of the 1920s and 1930s in Fiction and in Autobiography." Speech presented to the Association for Education in Journalism Annual Convention, Athens, Ohio, July 1982. http://www.ijpc.org/uploads/files/DonnaBorn.

8. Berger, "Mary Coyle Chase," 66.

9. Berger, "Mary Coyle Chase."

CHAPTER 5: THE RAGING REPORTER

1. Berger, "Mary Coyle Chase," 15.

2. Robert L. Perkin, *The First Hundred Years: An Informal History of Denver and the Rocky Mountain News, 1859 to 1959* (Garden City: Doubleday, 1959), 458.

3. "Prohibition Inspired a New Generation of Women," Smithsonian Channel, June 23, 2017. https://www.youtube.com/Watch?v=EYKoOFluQEU.

4. Mary Coyle, "Charming Weddings Grace Past Week," *Rocky Mountain News*, July 11, 1926.

5. Charlie Wunder and Mary Coyle, "Charley and Mary Look Over Collitch Boys, Don't Like 'Em," *Rocky Mountain News*, March 13, 1927, 4.

6. Mary Coyle, "Whisperer's Campaign Rejected by Both Parties," *Rocky Mountain News*, September 30, 1928.

7. Mary Coyle, "Whisperer's Campaign."

8. Mary Coyle, "Whisperer's Campaign."

9. Melrose, "Reporter to Playwright," 8, 50.

10. Perkin, *One Hundred Years*, 459.

11. Perkin, *One Hundred Years*.

12. Perkin, *One Hundred Years*.

13. Perkin, *One Hundred Years*, 500.

14. Anne Comire, "Something About the Author," *National Cyclopedia*, Volume 17, 1979, 40.

15. Mary Chase, "City Room to Stage," *Rocky Mountain News*, April 19, 1959.

CHAPTER 6: SHE MEETS HER MAN

1. Perkin, *One Hundred Years*, 419.

2. Perkin, *One Hundred Years*, 495.

3. Perkin, *One Hundred Years*, 495.

4. Jerry Chase telephone interview by Mimi Pockross, April 4, 2018.

5. Perkin, *One Hundred Years*.

6. "Newspaper Romance Ends in Marriage of Reporters," *Rocky Mountain News*, June 8, 1928.

7. Mark Baron, "Mary Chase Doesn't Act Part of Broadway Playwright," *Rocky Mountain News*, October 26, 1952, 48.

8. Ward Morehouse, "Interview with Mary Chase," *The Sun*, North American Newspaper Alliance, July 17, 1946.

CHAPTER 7: THE HOUSEWIFE

1. Denver City and Householder Directories, Directory and Street Guide, 1935 to 1937, volumes 11–14.

2. Carolyn Casey Craig, *Women Pulitzer Playwrights: Biographical Profiles and Analyses of the Plays* (Jefferson, NC: McFarland & Company, Inc. 2004), 65.

3. Willingham, "Introduce Them to Harvey," 81.

4. Berger, "Mary Coyle Chase," 55.

5. Perkin, *One Hundred Years*, 499.

CHAPTER 8: THE FEDERAL THEATRE PROJECT

1. Hallie Flanagan, "Is This the Time and Place?" Delivered to the First Meeting of Regional Theater Directors-Federal Theatre Project, Washington, DC, October 8, 1935. https://www.loc.gov/item/farbf.00010001/.

2. Flanagan, "Is This the Time and Place?"

3. Chase to Wickre.

4. Chase to Wickre.

5. Chase to Wickre.

6. Chase to Wickre.

7. A. Pike, "Me Third in Denver," *Rocky Mountain News*, November 28, 1936.

8. A. De Bernardi, Jr., "Farce by Local Writer," *Denver Post*, November 28, 1936.

9. Chase to Wickre.

10. Chase to Wickre.

11. Willingham, "Introduce Them to Harvey," 39.

CHAPTER 9: THE BROADWAY FLOP

1. Berger, "Mary Coyle Chase," 20.

2. Chase to Wickre.

3. Ellis Nassour, "Remembering Tony Namesake Antoinette Perry," *Special Tony Playbill*, June 4, 1998. http://playbill.com/tonynamesake-antoinette-perry-com-75756.

4. Bosley Crowther, "The Lady in the Cage," *New York Times*, March 14, 1937, Sec. 11, p. 1.

5. Nassour, "Remembering Tony."

6. Willingham, "Introduce Them to Harvey," 49.

7. Brooks Atkinson, "The Play: Now You've Done It," *New York Times*, March 6, 1937.

8. "Brock Pemberton," ed. Anna Rothe, *Current Biography*, 1945.

9. Chase to Wickre.

10. Mary Chase, "My Life with Harvey," *McCalls*, February 1951, 56.

11. "News and Gossip of Broadway," *New York Times*, December 27, 1936, 1–2.

12. Chase to Wickre.

13. Chase to Wickre.

14. Atkinson, "Now You've Done It."

15. Willingham, "Introduce Them to Harvey," 54.

16. Douglas Gilbert, "Now You've Done It," *New York World Telegram*, March 5, 1937.

17. Reef, "She Didn't Write It For The Money."

18. Robert Benchley, "Science and Other Matters," *New Yorker*, March 13, 1937.

19. "Theatre: Meat Show Meeting," *Time*, June 7, 1937, 26.

20. Frances Melrose, "Mrs. Chase Pleased with Care of 'Harvey,'" *Rocky Mountain News*, February 28, 1977, 8.

21. Duncan Clark, "Harvey's Mom," *Rocky Mountain News*, July 6, 1947, 21–22.

22. Chase to Wickre.

23. Chase to Wickre.

24. Berger, "Mary Coyle Chase" 21.

CHAPTER 10: TIME TO REGROUP

1. A. De Bernardi, Jr., "Sorority House Is Keen Satire," *Denver Post*, October 28, 1938.

2. Frank S. Nugent, "The Screen," review of "Sorority House," *The New York Times*, May 18, 1939. https://www.nytimes.com/1939/05/18/archives/the-screen.html.

CHAPTER 11: THE POOKA

1. Angela Colley, "Top 10 Irish Myths and Legends," *TopTenz*, March 17, 2011. https://www.toptenz.net/top-10-irish-myths-and-legends.php.
2. Chase, "My Life," 54.

CHAPTER 12: BACK TO BROADWAY

1. John L. Toohey, *A History of the Pulitzer Prize Plays* (New York: Citadel Press, 1967), 198.
2. Willingham, "Introduce Them to Harvey,"103.
3. Berger, "Mary Coyle Chase," 35.
4. Berger, "Mary Coyle Chase," 109.
5. Mary Chase, *Harvey* (New York: Dramatists Play Service, 1950), Act 3, 64. Rewrite explanation comes from Murdock Pemberton, "Brock Pemberton: Man of the Theatre," *New York Times*, March 19, 1950, section 2:1.
6. Robert L. Chase Papers.
7. Melrose, "Reporter to Playwright."
8. Chase, "My Life."
9. Willingham, "Introduce Them to Harvey," 112.
10. Chase, "My Life," 56.
11. Chase, *Harvey*, Act 1, Scene 2, 33.

CHAPTER 13: IT'S A HIT!

1. Chase, *Harvey*, Act 1, Scene 1, 4.
2. Chase, *Harvey*, Act 1, Scene 1, 5.
3. Chase, *Harvey*.
4. Chase, *Harvey*, Act 2, Scene 1, 38.
5. Chase, *Harvey*, Act 1, Scene 2, 54.
6. Chase, *Harvey*, Act 2, Scene 1, 44.
7. Chase, *Harvey*, Act 3, 69.
8. Chase, "My Life."
9. John Chapman, "Harvey," *New York Daily News*, November 11, 1944.
10. "The Invisible Rabbit," *Time*, November 13, 1944.
11. Burton Rascoe, "Harvey," *New York World Telegram*, November 11, 1944.
12. Craig, *Women Pulitzer Playwrights*, 98.
13. Melrose, "Mrs. Chase Pleased."
14. Abe Laufe, *Anatomy of a Hit* (New York: Hawthorne Books, Inc., 1966), 168–69.

15. Laufe, *Anatomy of a Hit*, 69.

16. Melrose, "Mrs. Chase Pleased," 9.

17. Clark, "Harvey's Mom."

18. "Harvey," *Playbill*, November 1, 1944, 18.

19. Phil Goodstein, *Magnificent Mayfair, Beautiful Bellevue, Hale, Hilltop, Hospitals: The Story of Modern East Denver* (Denver, CO: New Social Publications 2017).

20. Louis Kronenberger, "Harvey," *PM Magazine*, November 2, 1944.

21. "Harvey," Roundabout Theatre, https://www.roundabouttheatre.org/get-tickets /2011-2012-season/harvey/.

CHAPTER 14: A NEW REALITY

1. Chase, "My Life."

2. Chase, "My Life."

3. Hugh McGovern, "1945 Was Year for Mary Chase," *Denver Post*, December 9, 1951, 3.

4. Chase, "My Life."

5. Chase, "My Life."

6. Mary Coyle Chase, "And a Rabbit Caused It All," *Rocky Mountain News*, July 11, 1945, 23.

7. Eleanor Harris, "Success Almost Ruined Her," *Cosmopolitan*, February, 1954, 102.

8. Clark, "Harvey's Mom," 21.

9. Robert Chase Papers.

10. Robert Chase Papers.

11. "Traveling Chase Family Returns: Harvey Could Be Anywhere," *Rocky Mountain News*, April 24, 1947.

12. Robert Chase Papers.

13. Clark, "Harvey's Mom."

CHAPTER 15: THE PULITZER PRIZE

1. Lee Casey, "Mary Coyle Chase Winning Pulitzer Prize Makes Mary Chase's Dream a Reality," *Rocky Mountain News*, May 9, 1945, 15.

2. Seymour Topping, "The History of the Pulitzer Prizes," additional editing by Sig Gissler, *The Pulitzer Prizes.org*. https://www.pulitzer.org/page/history-pulitzer-prizes.

3. Toohey, *A History of the Pulitzer Prize Plays*, 200.

4. Heinz-Dietrich Fischer, *Outstanding Broadway Dramas and Comedies: Pulitzer Prize Winning Theater* (Munster, Germany: LIT Verlag, 2013), 60.

5. Paul A. Firestone, *The Pulitzer Prize Plays, The First Fifty Years, 1917 to 1967: A Dramatic Reflection of American Life*, edited by Paul Firestone (Milwaukee, WI: Hal Leonard, Limelight Editions, 2008), 313.

6. Laufe, *Anatomy of a Hit*, 168.

7. Melrose, "Mrs. Chase Pleased."

8. "History," *New York Drama Critics' Circle Since 1935.* https://www.dramacritics.org/dc_history.html

9. Firestone, "A Dramatic Reflection of American Life."

10. Firestone, "A Dramatic Reflection of American Life."

11. Chase, "My Life," 58.

CHAPTER 16: HOLLYWOOD

1. Andrea Passafiume, *Harvey* (1950), TCM *Turner Classic Movies.* https://www.tcm.com/tcmdb/title/19347/Harvey/articles.html.

2. Passafiume, "Harvey (1950)."

3. *Harvey.* American Film Institute. www.AFI.com.

4. Passafiume, "Harvey (1950)."

5. Barbara MacKay, "Mary Chase, Colorado's Lady of the Theatre," *Bravo Magazine,* Denver Center for the Performing Arts, December 1981, Vol. 5, No. 12, 17.

6. Passafiume, "Harvey (1950)."

7. Chase to Wickre.

8. Andrea Passafiume and Jeffrey Stafford, "The Critics' Corner," *Harvey* (1950), TCM, *Turner Classic Movies.* https://www.tcm.com/tcmdb/title/19347/Harvey/articles.html.

CHAPTER 17: SETTLING DOWN

1. Melrose, "Mrs. Chase Pleased," 8.

2. Harris, "Success Almost Ruined Her," 104.

3. Robert Chase Papers.

4. Tom and Susan Hilb interview by Mimi Pockross, Denver, Colorado, April 3, 2018.

5. Chase "My Life."

CHAPTER 18: NEW BEGINNINGS

1. Harris, "Success Almost Ruined Her," 102.

2. Harris, "Success Almost Ruined Her."

3. Baron, "Mary Chase Doesn't Act Part."

4. John Chapman, "Mrs. McThing: A Play in Two Acts," in *The Best Plays 1951–52,* edited by John Chapman (New York: Dodd, Mead 1952).

5. Hilb interview.

6. Mary Chase, "Playwriting Tips from Small Fry," *New York Times,* February 17, 1952, section 2:1.

7. "Mrs. McThing," *Playbill,* Central City, Colorado, August 1952.

8. "Mrs. McThing."

9. Richard Watts, Jr., "Two on the Aisle," *New York Post,* March 2, 1952.

10. "Mrs. McThing."

11. Joanna Krauss, "Mary Coyle Chase (1907–1981)," encyclopedia.com, November 13, 2018. https://www.encyclopedia.com/women/encyclopedias-almanacs-transcripts-and-maps/chase-mary-coyle-1907-1981.

12. Watts, "Two on the Aisle."

13. Berger, "Mary Coyle Chase," 136.

14. "My Day," Eleanor Roosevelt, United Features Syndicate (Chicago, Illinois), June 15, 1952.

15. "Mrs. McThing."

16. Chapman, *The Best Plays of 1951–52.*

17. "Bernardine Shamrock Snug," *Denver Post*, June 19, 1957, 28.

18. Mary Chase, *Bernardine* (United Kingdom: Oxford Press, 1953) (revised edition, New York: Dramatists Play Service, 1954), 1.

19. Willingham, "Introduce Them to Harvey," 144.

20. Willingham, "Introduce Them to Harvey."

21. Willingham, "Introduce Them to Harvey."

22. Baron, "Mary Chase Doesn't Act the Part."

23. Robert Chase Papers.

CHAPTER 19: TELEVISION

1. William Forsche, "Jimmy Stewart Introduces Us to *Harvey*, Recorded in 1990 for the Home Video Release," youtube.com, March 31, 2013. https://www.youtube.com/watch?v=GVIAHBe4E7Q+t=299s.

CHAPTER 20: LADIES FIRST

1. Harris, "Success Almost Ruined Her," 101.

2. Mary Chase, *Loretta Mason Potts* (Philadelphia, PA: Lippincott, 1958) (revised edition, New York: New York Review Children's Collection, 2014).

3. Chase, *Loretta Mason Potts.*

4. Robert L. Chase Papers, letter sent to Lippincott Publishing.

5. John Chapman, "*Midgie Purvis* Review," *New York Times*, February 2, 1961.

6. Chapman, "*Midgie Purvis* Review."

7. Melrose, "Reporter to Playwright," 8, 50.

8. *Midgie Purvis*, Act I, Scene 4 (New York: Dramatists Play Service), 34.

9. Willingham, "Introduce Them to Harvey," 164.

10. Mary Chase and Henry Lowenstein, "Wicked Wicked Ladies" Correspondence, 1974–1976, Henry Lowenstein Papers, 1915–2004, Denver Public Library.

CHAPTER 21: PROFESSOR MARY

1. Berger, "Mary Coyle Chase," 53.

2. Berger, "Mary Coyle Chase," 34.

3. Mary Chase, University of Denver Class Notes, Mary Chase Papers, Spring Quarter, 1966, University of Denver Special Collections.

4. Mary Chase, "The Practice of Playwriting," *The Writer*, 18.

5. Clark, "Harvey's Mom."

6. Berger, "Mary Coyle Chase," 49.

7. Berger, "Mary Coyle Chase," 47.

8. Hilb interview.

9. Berger, "Mary Coyle Chase."

10. Berger, "Mary Coyle Chase," 46.

11. Berger, "Mary Coyle Chase," 40–41.

12. Berger, "Mary Coyle Chase," 42.

CHAPTER 22: AGELESS *HARVEY*

1. Melrose, "Mary Chase Pleased," 9.

2. Patricia Collins, "Harvey at Bonfils," *Denver Post*, December 11, 1978, 26.

3. Collins, "Harvey at Bonfils."

4. Lynn Gardner, "It Takes a Delusional Rabbit-Lover to See the Truth," *The Guardian*, February 15, 2018, 58. https://www.theguardian.com/stage/2015/feb/18/harvey-review-birmingham-repertory-theatre-lindsay-posner-revival.

5. Anna Chandler, "Collective Face Goes Down the Rabbit Hole with *Harvey*," *Connect Savannah*, November 29, 2017. https://www.connectsavannah.com/savannah/collective-face-goes-down-the-rabbit-hole/content?oid=6418314.

6. "Harvey-Opening Night," youtube.com, June 14, 2012. https://www.youtube.com/watch?v=BMICSenJFQ.

7. Jacqueline Terrebone, "The Sets of *Harvey* on Broadway," *Architectural Digest*, December 31, 2011. https://www.architecturaldigest.com/story/david-rockwell-harvey-sets-broadway-article.

8. David Rooney, "Harvey: Theater Review," *The Hollywood Reporter*, June 14, 2012. https://www.hollywoodreporter.com/review/harvey-theater-review-337880.

9. "Harvey Connections," IMDb.com. https:www.imdb.com/title/tt0042546/.

10. "Harvey Connections."

CHAPTER 23: *HARVEY*, THE MUSICAL

1. MacKay, "Colorado's Lady of the Theatre."

2. Jerry Chase phone interview.

3. Symons interview.

4. Laura Shamas, "When My Mom Had Tea With Mary Chase," *Los Angeles Female Playwrights Initiative*, December 13, 2015. http://lafpi.com/2015/12/when-my-mom-had-tea-with-mary-chase/.

5. Clifford Ridley, "Cozy Barter Mounts an Unfunny Little 'Mimi,'" *National Observer*, July 14, 1973.

6. Willingham, "Introduce Them to Harvey," 171.

7. Willingham, "Introduce Them to Harvey."

8. Willingham, "Introduce Them to Harvey."

9. "Say Hello to Harvey—1981 Broadway-Backstage & Production Info." https://www.broadwayworld.com/shows/backstage.php?showid=7034#contentstart.

10. Leslie Bricusse, "Say Hello to Harvey," Leslie Bricusse Stage. http://lesliebricusse.com/stage/stage_detail.php?id=18.

11. Ken Mandelbaum, *Not Since Carrie: Forty Years of Broadway Musical Flops* (New York: St. Martin's Griffin, 1991).

12. Ron Fassler, "Say Hello to Harvey," *Theatre Yesterday and Today*, medium.com, December 5, 2017. http://medium.com/@ronfassler/say-hell-to-harvey.

CHAPTER 24: THE CURTAIN FALLS

1. Herbert Mitgang, "Mary Chase, Playwright Who Wrote Harvey, Dead," *New York Times*, October 21, 1981, 18.

2. Barbara MacKay, "Harvey Author Dies," *Denver Post*, October 21, 1981.

3. Reef, "She Didn't Write It for the Money," 109.

4. Harris, "Success Almost Ruined Her," 104.

5. Harris, "Success Almost Ruined Her."

6. Lee Casey, "Our Mary," *Rocky Mountain News*, May 9, 1955.

7. Baron, "Mrs. Chase Doesn't Act the Part."

8. Michael Chase speech delivered at the Colorado Performing Arts Hall of Fame, Denver, Colorado, November 5, 1999. Marilyn Griggs Riley Papers. Denver Public Library.

9. Harris, "Success Almost Ruined Her."

10. Hilb interview.

11. Berger, "Mary Coyle Chase," 194.

12. Morehouse, "Interview with Mary Chase."

13. Melrose, "Mrs. Chase Pleased."

14. Berger, "Mary Coyle Chase," 34.

15. Berger, "Mary Coyle Chase," 12.

16. Harris, "Success Almost Ruined Her," 104

17. Chase, "My Life," 53.

18. McGovern, "1945 Was the Year," 3.

19. Chase, "My Life," 58.

20. Berger, "Mary Coyle Chase," 36.

21. Chase, "My Life," 57–58.

22. Frances Melrose, "Mary Chase's Fairy Story Delightful," *Rocky Mountain News*, August 23, 1960, 33.

23. Mary Chase, *Midgie Purvis* (New York: Dramatists Play Service, 1963).

CHAPTER 25: THE FINAL REVIEW

1. Craig, *Women Playwrights*, 100.

2. Chris Jones, "Play about Elwood and His Unseen Rabbit is a Story We Need to Believe In," *Chicago Tribune*, May 22, 2017. https://www.chicagotribune.com...theater/.../ct-harvey-court-review-ent-0523-20170.

3. Albert Wertheim, "The Comic Muse of Mary Chase," in *Women in American Theatre*, edited by Helen Krich Chinoy and Linda Walsh Jenkins (New York: Theater Communications Group, Crown 1987), 121–22.

4. Heather Addison, "The Dream Behind the Reality: Amiable Lunacy and Blithe Brutality in Harvey," *Bright Lights Film Journal*, June 17, 2014. https://brightlightsfilm.com/dream-behind-reality-amiable-lunacy-blithe-brutality-harvey/#XLSsPi-ZPwc.

5. Sherwin, Mary, ed., *Comedy Tonight: Broadway Picks Its Favorite Plays* (Garden City, NY: Doubleday, 1977).

6. Patrick Healy, "High Spirited Comedies Rush the Stage," *New York Times*, February 18, 2015. https://www.nytimes.com/2015/02/22/.../high-spirited-comedies-rush-the-stage.html.

7. Katherine A. Fowkes, "Harvey: A Happy Hallucination?" *The Fantasy Film* (Hoboken, NJ: Wiley-Blackwell, 2010), 68–80.

8. David W. Sievers, "New Freudian Blood," in *Freud on Broadway: A History of Psychoanalysis and the American Drama*, edited by David W. Sievers (New York: Hermitage House, 1955). https://www.enotes.com/topics/mary-coyle-chase.

9. Krauss, "Mary Coyle Chase (1907–1981)."

10. Wertheim, "The Comic Muse of Mary Chase," 121.

11. Wertheim, "The Comic Muse of Mary Chase."

12. Addison, "The Dream Behind the Reality."

13. Chase to Wickre.

14. Toohey, *A History of the Pulitzer Prize Plays*, 199.

15. "Harvey," https://www.enotes.com/topics/harvey/critical-essays.

16. Wertheim, "The Comic Muse of Mary Chase," 121–22.

17. Wertheim, "The Comic Muse of Mary Chase."

18. Walter Kerr, "Remembrances of Things Past," in *The God on the Gymnasium Floor*, edited by Walter Kerr (New York: Simon and Schuster, 1971).

19. Jones, "Play about Elwood."

20. "Harvey." Roundabout Theatre. www.roundabouttheatre.org.

21. Wertheim, "The Comic Muse of Mary Chase."

22. McGovern, "1945 Was Year for Mary Chase."

23. McGovern, "1945 Was Year for Mary Chase."

BIBLIOGRAPHY

Addison, Heather. "The Dream Behind the Reality: Amiable Lunacy and Blithe Brutality in Harvey." *Bright Lights Film Journal*, June 17, 2014.

Archer, William. *Playmaking: A Manual of Craftsmanship*. London: Chapman and Hall, 1912. Revised edition: New Haven, CT: Yale University, 2004.

Atkinson, Brooks. "The Play: Now You've Done It." *New York Times*, March 6, 1937.

"Author, Film Star Meet at Bernardine Premier." *Rocky Mountain News*, June 22, 1957.

"Baker Historic District." www.denvergov.org.

Caroline Bancroft Family Papers. Denver Public Library.

Baron, Mark. "Mary Chase Doesn't Act Part of Broadway Playwright." *Rocky Mountain News*, October 26, 1952.

Barrett, Marjorie. "Mary Chase's 1st Book." *Rocky Mountain News*, September 24, 1958.

Benchley, Robert. "Science and Other Matters." *New Yorker*, March 13, 1937.

Berger, Maurice Albert. "Mary Coyle Chase: Her Battlefield of Illusion." PhD dissertation. Denver, Colorado, University of Denver, August 1970.

"Bernardine Shamrock Snug." *Denver Post*, June 19, 1957.

Born, Donna. "The Woman Journalist of the 1920s and 1930s in Fiction and in Autobiography," July 1982. www.ijpc.org.

Boylan, Jennifer Finney. "My Favorite Holiday Movie Involves a Giant Rabbit." *New York Times*, December 12, 2017.

Bricusse, Leslie. "Say Hello to Harvey." www.lesliebricussestage.com.

Casey, Lee. "Our Mary." *Rocky Mountain News*, May 9, 1945.

———. "Mary Coyle Chase Winning Pulitzer Prize Makes Mary Chase's Dream a Reality." *Rocky Mountain News*, May 9, 1945, 15.

Catlett, Sharon R. *Farmlands, Forts and Country Life: The Story of Southwest Denver*. Denver, CO: Westcliffe Publishers, 2007.

Cervi, Clé, and Nancy Peterson. *The Women Who Made the Headlines*. Denver, CO: Western Guideways, 1998.

Chapman, John, "Mrs. McThing." In *The Best Plays of 1951–52*, edited by John Chapman. New York: Dodd, Mead, 1952.

———. "Harvey Review." *New York Daily News*, November 2, 1944.

———. "Midgie Purvis Review." *New York Times*, February 2, 1961.

Chandler, Anna. "Collective Face Down the Rabbit Hole with *Harvey*." *Connect Savannah*, November 19, 2017. www.savannahconnect.com.

"Chase Family Travels to London." *Rocky Mountain News*, February 1, 1947.

Chase, Mary. "And a Rabbit Caused it All. My Life Exploded." *Rocky Mountain News*, July 11, 1945.

———. *Bernardine*. New York: Dramatists Play Service, 1954.

———. "City Room to Stage." *Rocky Mountain News*, April 19, 1959.

———. "Class notes." Spring Quarter 1966. University of Denver Special Collections.

———. *The Dog Sitters*. New York: Dramatists Play Service, 1963.

———. *Harvey*. New York: Dramatists Play Service, 1950.

———. "He's Our Baby." *McCall's*, April,1945.

———. *Loretta Mason Potts*. Illustrated by Harold Berson. Philadelphia, PA: Lippincott, 1958.

———. *Mrs. McThing*. Rev. ed. New York: Dramatists Play Service, 1954.

———. *Midgie Purvis*. New York: Dramatists Play Service, 1963.

———. "My Life with Harvey." *McCall's*, February 1951.

———. "Playwriting Tips From Small Fry." *New York Times*, February 17, 1952.

———. "Recollections of a Colorado Newswoman." *Colorado Editor*, December 1958.

———. "The Halloween World of Youth." *New York Times*, November 23, 1952.

———. "The Practice of Playwriting." *The Writer*, June 1963.

———. "The White Rabbit." Special Collections, University of Denver: unpublished, 1944.

Chase, Jerry telephone interview by Mimi Pockross, April 4, 2018.

Chase, Michael. Speech delivered at the Colorado Performing Arts Hall of Fame, Denver, Colorado, November 5, 1999. Marilyn Griggs Riley Papers, Denver Public Library.

Robert Lamont Chase Papers, 1915–1986. Denver Public Library Western History Department.

Clark, Duncan. "Harvey's Mom." *Rocky Mountain News*, July 6, 1947.

Colley, Angela. "Top 10 Irish Myths and Legends." www.toptenz.net.

Collins, Patricia. "Harvey at Bonfils." *Denver Post*, December 11, 1978.

Comire, Anne. "Something About the Author." In *National Cyclopedia*, 1979, Volume 17, 40.

Coyle, Mary. "Charming Weddings Grace Past Week." *Rocky Mountain News*, July 11, 1926.

———. "Whisperer's Campaign Rejected by Both Parties." *Rocky Mountain News*, September 30, 1938.

Craig, Carolyn Casey. *Women Pulitzer Playwrights: Biographical Profiles and Analyses of the Plays*. Jefferson, NC: McFarland & Company, Inc., 2004.

Crowther, Bosley. "The Lady in the Cage." *New York Times*, March 14, 1937.

De Bernardi Jr., A. "Farce by Local Writer." *Denver Post*, November 28, 1936.

———. "Sorority House is Keen Satire." *Denver Post*, October 28, 1937.

"Denver: Curtis Street—Denver's Old Theater Row." December 5, 2010. www.forum skyscraper.com.

Denver City and Householder Directories, 1935–1937. Denver Public Library.

Erdman, Andrew L. "Mary Coyle Chase: A Bibliography of Critical and Biographical Sources." *Bulletin of Bibliography*, Volume 52, December 1995.

Fassler, Ron. "Say Hello to Harvey." *Theatre Yesterday and Today*, December 5, 2017.

Firestone, Paul A. *The Pulitzer Prize Plays: The First 50 Years: 1916–1967: A Dramatic Reflection of American Life*. New York: Hal Leonard, 2008, 313.

Fischer, Heinz-Dietrich. *Outstanding Broadway Dramas and Comedies: Pulitzer Prize Winning Theater*. Munster, Germany: LIT Verlag, 2013, 60.

Flanagan, Hallie. "Is This the Time and Place?" Delivered to the First Meeting of Regional Theater Directors—Federal Theatre Project. Washington, DC: Library of Congress. October 8, 1935.

Forsche, William. "Jimmy Stewart Introduces us to Harvey, recorded in 1990 for the Home Video Release." March 31, 2013.

Fowkes, Katharine A. *The Fantasy Film*. Hoboken, NJ: Wiley-Blackwell, 2010, 68–80.

Fowler, Gene. *Timberline A Story of Bonfils and Tammen*. New York: Covici Friede, 1933.

Gardner, Lynn. "It Takes a Delusional Rabbit-Lover to See the Truth." *The Guardian*, February 18, 2015.

Gilbert, Douglas. "Now You've Done It." *New York World Telegram*, March 5, 1937.

Goodstein, Phil. *Magnificent Mayfair, Beautiful Bellevue, Hilltop, Hospitals: The Story of Modern East Denver*. Denver, CO: New Social Publications, 2017.

Harris, Eleanor. "Success Almost Ruined Her." *Cosmopolitan*, February 1954.

"Harvey."
www.AFI.com
www.broadwayworld.com
www.enotes.com/topics/harvey/critical-essays
www.IMDb.com
www.playbill.com
www.roundabouttheatre.org
www.shawfestival.com
www.tcm.com
www.wikipedia.org

"Harvey." 48th Street Theatre *Playbill*, 1944.

"Harvey – Opening Night," youtube.com. June 14, 2012. https://www.youtube.com/watch?v=BMICSenJFQ.

Healy, Patrick. "High-Spirited Comedies Rush the Stage." *New York Times*, February 18, 2015.

Hilb, Tom and Susan interview by Mimi Pockross, Denver, Colorado, April 3, 2018.

"History, New York." Drama Critics Circle since 1935. http://www.dramacritics.org.

"Louise Sneed Hill and Denver's Sacred Thirty-Six." https://fairmount-cemetery.com/louise-sneed-hill-and-denvers-sacred-thirty-six, April 23, 2013.

Jones, Chris. "Play about Elwood and His Unseen Rabbit is a Story We Need to Believe In." *Chicago Tribune*, May 22, 2017.

Kerr, Walter. "Remembrances of Things Past," in *The God on the Gymnasium Floor*, edited by Walter Kerr. New York: Simon and Schuster, 1971.

Kline, Hebron Charles. "A History of Denver Theater During the Depression Era, 1929 to 1941," Thesis, University of Denver, 1963.

"Henry Koster and Jimmy Stewart." www.silverscenes.blogspot.com

Krauss, Joanna. "Mary Coyle Chase (1907–1981)." www.encyclopedia.com, November 13, 2018.

Kronenberger, Louis. "Harvey." *PM*, November 2, 1944.

Laufe, Abe. *Anatomy of a Hit*. New York: Hawthorne Books, Inc., 1966, 168–69.

Leonard, Stephen J. *Trials and Triumphs: A Colorado Portrait of the Great Depression with FSA Photographs*. Boulder: University of Colorado Press, 1993.

———— and Thomas J. Noel. *Denver: Mining Camp to Metropolis*. Boulder: University of Colorado Press, 1991.

————. *A Short History of Denver*. Reno, NV: University of Nevada Press, 2016.

Henry Lowenstein Papers 1915–2004. Denver Public Library.

Mary Chase interview with Alan B. Fisher, Fisher and Fisher Architectural Records and Correspondence, undated. Denver Public Library.

MacKay, Barbara. "Mary Chase, Colorado's Lady of Theatre." *Bravo Magazine*, Denver Center for the Performing Arts, December 1981, Vol. 5, No. 12.

————. "Harvey Author Dies," *Denver Post*, October 21, 1981.

Mandelbaum, Ken. *Not Since Carrie: 40 Years of Broadway Musical Flops*. New York: St. Martin's Griffin, 1991.

McGovern, Hugh. "1945 Was Year for Mary Chase." *Denver Post*, December 9, 1951.

Melrose, Frances. "Mary Chase's Fairy Story Delightful." *Rocky Mountain News*, August 23, 1960.

————. "Mary Chase: Reporter to Playwright." *Rocky Mountain News*, February 27, 1977.

————. "Mrs. Chase Pleased with Care of 'Harvey.'" *Rocky Mountain News*, February 28, 1977.

————. "Mary Chase Takes Broadway Bulls-eye Calmly." *Rocky Mountain News*, November 7, 1944.

Metzinger, Constance and Diana. "Director Henry Koster and Jimmy Stewart," January 23, 2016. https://silverscenesblog.blogspot.com.

Miller, Frank. "The Great White Way of Denver's Theater Row." *The Denver Post Archive*, May 28, 2013.

Mitgang, Herbert. "Mary Chase." *New York Times*, October 23, 1981.

Morehouse, Ward. "Interview with Mary Chase." North American Newspaper Alliance, *New York World Telegram and Sun*, July 17, 1946.

Morris, Elizabeth J. K. "A History of the Denver Center Theater, 1929 to 1968," master's thesis, University of Colorado, Boulder, 1968.

"Mrs. McThing." Central City *Playbill*, 1952.

"Mrs. McThing Premiere." *Life Magazine*, March 10, 1952.

Nassour, Ellis. "Remembering Tony Namesake Antoinette Perry." *Special Tony Playbill*, June 4, 1998.

"News and Gossip of Broadway." *New York Times*, December 27, 1936.

"Newspaper Romance Ends in Marriage of Reporters." *Rocky Mountain News*, June 8, 1928.

Noel, Thomas J. "Mary Chase." In *Scribner Encyclopedia of American Lives*, Volume 1: 1982–1985.

———— and Amy B. Zimmer. *Showtime: Denver's Performing Arts, Convention Centers and Theatre District*. Denver, CO: Denver's Division of Theatres & Arenas, 2008.

Nugent, Frank. "The Screen," review of "Sorority House." *New York Times*, May 18, 1939.

"Opening Night of Harvey Starring Jim Parsons," www.youtube.com, June 14, 2012.

Passafiume, Andrea. "Harvey (1950)." TCM *Turner Classic Movies*. https://www.tcm.com.

Passafiume, Andrea and Jeffrey Stafford. "The Critics' Corner," *Harvey (1950), TCM Turner Classic Movies*. https://www.tcm.com.

Pemberton, Murdock. "Brock Pemberton: Man of the Theatre." *New York Times*, March 19, 1950.

Perkin, Robert L. *The First Hundred Years: An Informal History of Denver and the Rocky Mountain News, 1859 to 1959*. Forward by Gene Fowler. Garden City: Doubleday 1959, 419–544.

Pike, A. "Me Third in Denver." *Rocky Mountain News*, November 28, 1936.

"Prohibition Inspired a New Generation of Women." *Smithsonian Channel*, June 23, 2017. https://www.youtube.com.

Rascoe, Burton. "Harvey Review." *New York World Telegram*, November 2, 1944.

Reef, Wallace. "She Didn't Write It for Money—She Says." *Saturday Evening Post*, September 1, 1945.

Ridley, Clifford. "Cozy Barter Mounts an Unfunny Little 'Mimi.'" *National Observer*, July 14, 1973.

Riley, Marilyn Griggs. *High Altitude Attitudes: Six Savvy Colorado Women*. Boulder, CO: Big Earth Publishing, Johnson Books, 2006.

Roosevelt, Eleanor. "My Day." United Features Syndicate, June 15, 1952.

Rothe, Anna, ed. "Brock Pemberton." In *Current Biography*. New York: H.W. Wilson, 1945.

———. "Mary Coyle." In *Current Biography*. New York: H.W. Wilson, 1945.

"Say Hello to Harvey." www.broadwayworld.com.

Shakespeare, William. "Macbeth." *The Complete Works of William Shakespeare*, Lea edition, Michael Cramer, Phd, author. California: Canterbury Classics, 2014.

Shamas, Laura. "When My Mom Had Tea with Mary Chase." December 13, 2015. http://lafpi.com/2015/12/when-my-mom-had-tea-with-mary-chase/.

Sherwin, Mary, ed. *Comedy Tonight: Broadway Picks Its Favorite Plays*. Garden City, New York: Doubleday, 1977.

Sievers, David W. "New Freudian Blood." In *Freud on Broadway: A History of Psychoanalysis and the American Drama*, edited by David W. Sievers. New York: Hermitage House, 1955.

Sorotick, Marsha. "Mary Chase: The Woman Behind Harvey." *Irish America*, October 1, 2016.

Symons, Clé Cervi interview by Mimi Pockross, Denver, Colorado, November 30, 2017.

"Tabor Grand Opera House." www.cinematreasures.org.

"Tales of the Pooka." www.irelandofthewelcomes.com.

"Television." www.wikipedia.com.

"Television Shows." https://www.tvcom/.

Terrebone, Jacqueline. "The Sets of *Harvey* on Broadway." *Architectural Digest*, December 31, 2011.

"The Invisible Rabbit," *Time Magazine*, November 13, 1944.

"The Roaring Twenties History." *A&E TV Network*, April 4, 2010.

"Theatre: Meat Show Meeting." *Time Magazine*, June 7, 1937.

"Timeline of U.S. History (1900–1929)." www.wikipedia.com.

Toohey, John L. *A History of the Pulitzer Prize Plays*. New York: The Citadel Press, 1967, 199–200.

Topping, Seymour, "The History of the Pulitzer Prizes," ed. Sig Gissler. https://www.pulitzer.org.

"Traveling Chase Family Returns: Harvey Could be Almost Anywhere." *Rocky Mountain News*, April 24, 1947.

Vervalin, Gene. *A Walk on the West Side: The Story of an American High School*. Boulder, CO: EHV Publications, 1985.

Watts, Jr., Richard. "Two on the Aisle." *New York Post*, March 2, 1952.

Wertheim, Albert. "The Comic Muse of Mary Chase." In *Women in American Theatre*, edited by Helen Krich Chinoy and Linda Walsh Jenkins. New York: Theatre Communications Group, Crown, 1987, 162.

Willingham, Ralph. "Introduce Them to Harvey: Mary Chase and the Theatre," master's thesis, Commerce, TX: East Texas University, 1987.

Wunder, Charlie, and Mary Coyle. "Charlie and Mary Look Over Collitch Boys, Don't Like 'Em." *Rocky Mountain News*, March 13, 1927.

Zolotow, Maurice. "Frank Fay." *Life Magazine*, January 8, 1945.

INDEX

Page references for photos are italicized.

PHOTO CREDITS

Photo page 1, top: From the Denver Public Library, Western History Collection [WH995]. Used with permission.

Photo page 1, bottom: From the Denver Public Library, Western History Collection. Used with permission.

Photo page 2, top: From the Harry Rhoads Collection, the Denver Public Library, Western History Collection [Rh-5941]. Used with permission.

Photo page 2, bottom: MS Thr 382 (318). Houghton Library, Harvard University. Used with permission.

Photo page 3, top: From the *Rocky Mountain News*, the Denver Public Library, Western History Collection [WH2129]. Used with permission.

Photo page 3, bottom: From the University of Denver Special Collections. Used with permission of Central City Opera.

Photo page 4, top: From L. Tom Perry Special Collections, Harold B. Lee Library, Brigham Young University. Used with permission.

Photo page 4, bottom: Photo by Talbot © Billy Rose Theatre Division, The New York Library for the Performing Arts. Used with permission.

Photo page 5, top: From the Denver Public Library, Western History Collection. Used with permission.

Photo page 5, bottom: From *The New York Review of Books*. Used with permission of Jed Feffer (estate of Harold Berson).

Photo page 6, top: From the *Rocky Mountain News* (photo by Bob Talkin), the Denver Public Library, Western History Collection [WH2129]. Used with permission.

Photo page 6, bottom: From the Denver Public Library, Western History Collection [WH1141]. Used with permission.

Photo page 7, top: From the Denver Public Library, Western History Collection [WH1141]. Used with permission.

Photo page 7, bottom: From the *Rocky Mountain News* (photo by Mel Schieltz), the Denver Public Library, Western History Collection [WH2129]. Used with permission.

Photo page 8, top: From the *Rocky Mountain News* (photo by Howard Brock), the Denver Public Library, Western History Collection [WH2129]. Used with permission.

Photo page 8, bottom: From the *Rocky Mountain News* (photo by William Thach), the Denver Public Library, Western History Collection [WH2129]. Used with permission.